Teaching and Learning on Foundation Degrees

A Guide for Tutors and Support Staff in Further and Higher Education

Claire Taylor

continuum

Continuum International Publishing Group

The Tower Building   80 Maiden Lane
11 York Road   Suite 704
London SE1 7NX   New York NY 10038

www.continuumbooks.com

© Claire Taylor and Contributors 2012

British Library Cataloguing-in-Publication Data
A catalogue record for this book is available from the British Library.

ISBN: 978-1-4411-0545-5 hardcover
       978-1-4411-9614-9 paperback

Library of Congress Cataloging-in-Publication Data
Taylor, Claire, 1968-
Teaching and learning on foundation degrees : a guide for tutors and
support staff in further and higher education / Claire Taylor.
   p. cm.
 Includes bibliographical references and index.
 ISBN 978-1-4411-0545-5 (hardcover) – ISBN 978-1-4411-9614-9 (pbk.)
– ISBN 978-1-4411-4763-9 (ebk. (ePub)) – ISBN 978-1-4411-2954-3
(ebk. (PDF))   1. University extension–Great Britain.   2. Education,
Cooperative–Great Britain.   3. Continuing education–Great Britain.
4. Educational equalization–Great Britain.   I. Title.

  LC6256.G7T39 2012
  374'.941–dc23

                        2011023004

Typeset by Newgen Imaging Systems Pvt Ltd, Chennai, India
Printed and bound in India

Contents

Notes on Contributors

David Barber is head of e-Learning at Bishop Grosseteste University College Lincoln, UK. Previously he worked for the Open University and the University of Wales, Swansea. His current research interests touch on many subjects relating to the use of technology in learning and teaching.

Angela House is coordinator of flexible and distributed learning at Bishop Grosseteste University College Lincoln, UK. She lectures on child development and early years across work-based programmes and is developing collaborative provision across the University College. Angela has worked in a variety of educational settings within the UK and internationally.

Hazel Kent is a learning developer at Bishop Grosseteste University College Lincoln, UK, working with students to develop and enhance the study skills, academic practices and attributes needed for independent and effective study in HE. Her background is as a secondary school teacher and HE tutor.

Sacha Mason is a lecturer at Bishop Grosseteste University College Lincoln, UK, working mainly with students following the FdA Children's Services (Early Years). She has taught in a variety of settings including within schools and FE.

Alison Riley is the academic coordinator for Early Childhood Studies at Bishop Grosseteste University College Lincoln, UK, working with students following the Foundation and Honours degree programmes. Previously she held a range of school-based roles, including as deputy headteacher and acting headteacher.

Jane Sharp is a learning developer at Bishop Grosseteste University College Lincoln, UK, working with students to develop and enhance the study techniques, academic practices and attributes needed for independent and effective study in HE. Her background is as a lecturer and researcher in the field of teacher education and ICT.

Claire Taylor is dean of Students and Academic Engagement at Bishop Grosseteste University College Lincoln, UK. She has worked with Foundation Degree students since 2002 and has research interests in the areas of work-based learning and the student experience.

Acknowledgements

There are a number of individuals who have contributed in many ways to this book. First and foremost, our thanks to the many Foundation Degree students who have allowed us to share in their learning journeys through further and higher education. In particular, thanks to those students who, although anonymous, have contributed their 'learner voice' at various points throughout this book. Our thanks also to colleagues at Bishop Grosseteste University College who have encouraged us through the process of writing and reflecting upon learning and teaching on Foundation Degrees. In particular, we are grateful to Shan Lewis-Hobbs and Jan Machalski who have contributed specific case study material. Finally, Rachael Burnett has supported us tirelessly with word-processing, proofreading and a multitude of other tasks that have ensured we have stayed 'on track'. Thank you, Rachael.

Introduction
Claire Taylor

Chapter Outline

This introduction will:

- outline the background to writing this book
- identify who the book is for
- explain how the book is organized
- give a brief overview of each chapter.

Background

Foundation Degrees have been part of the higher education landscape in England and Wales since 2001. As work-based courses they have provided an alternative route through higher education for those students looking for a relevant employment-based course and, as such, Foundation Degrees have contributed to widening access and participation in higher education. This book brings together the practical experience and scholarly insight into learning and teaching on Foundation Degrees, developed by a group of staff at Bishop Grosseteste University College Lincoln over nearly ten years. In this respect, we hope that this book will be used by colleagues across the further and higher education sectors as a tool for reflecting upon their current practice and for developing new ways of teaching and supporting learning on Foundation Degrees.

Who the book is for

This book is intended for all those involved in teaching and supporting learning on Foundation Degrees. It will be of relevance to Foundation Degree lecturers, programme leaders, course managers and department heads, as well as academic and professional support staff involved in staff development, learning development and e-learning. The book provides both an academic and a practical basis upon which to reflect upon current practice regarding learning and teaching on Foundation Degrees, but should also serve as a useful reference book for staff looking to develop new Foundation Degree programmes within their institution.

How the book is organized

The book aims to be a practical handbook with a scholarly edge for all those involved in teaching and supporting learning on Foundation Degrees within further and higher education settings. Throughout the book, over 30 **case study** examples and reflection points contextualize relevant theory and discussion points highlighted in the text. The **reflection points** in particular provide a mechanism for structuring reflection and development activities for staff involved in Foundation Degree design and delivery. In addition, the **learner voice** appears throughout, bringing a student perspective on some of the issues raised. Furthermore, **resources and tools** can be found within the appendices, for use with Foundation Degree students and staff.

Chapter overviews

The chapter order is designed to take readers through a logical 'journey' with regard to the Foundation Degree. In this respect, Chapters 1 and 2 provide fairly theoretical introductions to the Foundation Degree format and to work-based learning. The reader is then taken through a series of chapters that address particular issues with regard to teaching and supporting learning on Foundation Degrees, before a more holistic consideration of key issues and a look to the future is presented in Chapter 8.

Chapter 1: what is a Foundation Degree?

This chapter outlines the developmental background to the establishment of the Foundation Degree qualification and surveys significant changes to the UK higher education landscape since the 1960s. It explores the place of Foundation Degrees as a response to the 'knowledge-based economy', higher education expansion and to changing attitudes towards vocational learning. Finally, the distinctive features of the Foundation Degree, as outlined in the QAA Benchmark (2010), are explored.

Chapter 2: work-based learning

This chapter is built upon the premise that it is important for tutors and support staff to have a well-developed understanding of the nature of work-based learning to bring a robust intellectual rationale and fully thought through philosophical approach to Foundation Degree design and delivery. The chapter begins by presenting definitions of work-based learning and then discusses 'socially situated learning' and 'experiential learning' as key characteristics of work-based learning. The nature of knowledge in relation to work-based learning is explored, as is work-based learning in practice.

Chapter 3: issues for learners

The learning needs of Foundation Degree students are a focus for this chapter. Mechanisms are explored for supporting learners before, during and beyond their Foundation Degree studies and the role of learning development services is also explored. Consideration is given to the support of students with dyslexia and other specific learning differences.

Chapter 4: course design

This chapter will provide essential support for all those involved in the development and validation of Foundation Degrees. It provides a holistic view of course design and gives advice on the validation process. The management of quality issues is discussed and student engagement is addressed. Guidance is provided for how to manage employer engagement in Foundation Degree provision.

Chapter 5: teaching strategies

A variety of teaching strategies are considered within this chapter in the context of the specific needs of Foundation Degree students and the unique features of the Foundation Degree. A particular focus is a blended learning approach (using technology-enhanced learning as appropriate) that typically incorporates face-to-face contact at the higher education institution (HEI) or further education college (FEC), independent learning and learning in the workplace.

Chapter 6: e-learning

This chapter explores why e-learning is relevant to the Foundation Degree. It looks at ways in which learning technologies support employer engagement and how students engage with the virtual learning environment. A pedagogical basis for the use of learning technologies is discussed.

Chapter 7: assessment

This chapter provides an overview of assessment practice in higher education and examines how assessment can be linked to course design. It explores how the work-based learning experiences of Foundation Degree students can be maximized in the assessment process and presents an overview of the types of assessments that might be used. The chapter concludes by considering issues related to preparing students for assessment and for handling the feedback they receive.

Chapter 8: looking to the future

By drawing together issues identified throughout the book, this final chapter suggests ways to 'future-proof' the Foundation Degree student experience through an exploration of learning enablers and inhibitors.

Consideration is given to the future of Foundation Degrees through a deliberation of political changes to the further and higher education landscape.

Whether you work through this book in chapter order, or 'dip in and out' of particular chapters depending upon your circumstance and needs, I hope that this book proves to be a useful tool for reflecting upon and improving practice in relation to learning and teaching on Foundation Degrees.

References

QAA (2010), *Foundation Degree Qualification Benchmark.* Gloucester: QAA.

1 What is a Foundation Degree?

Claire Taylor

This chapter will:

- outline the developmental background to the establishment of the Foundation Degree qualification
- present a survey of the significant changes within the UK higher education landscape since the 1960s
- explore the place of Foundation Degrees as a response both to higher education expansion and to changing attitudes towards vocational learning
- outline the development of work-based learning within higher education as part of 'the new vocationalism' (Symes and McIntyre, 2000)
- present the unique features pertaining to the Foundation Degree model as described in the Foundation Degree benchmark statement (QAA, 2010).

The expansion of higher education and the emergence of Foundation Degrees

Foundation Degrees were introduced as a new higher education qualification to England and Wales during the academic year 2001–2002. They are situated at Level 5 of the Framework for Higher Education Qualifications (FHEQ) for England, Wales and Northern Ireland (QAA, 2008) and feature the integration of academic study and work-based learning as a central part of course design and delivery (DfES, 2004; QAA, 2010). The position of the Foundation Degree within the FHEQ is shown in Appendix 1.

The first Foundation Degree courses began in September 2001, but the rationale for their appearance can be traced to a variety of initiatives linked to the expansion of higher education, beginning with the Robbins Report (Committee on Higher Education, 1963) which made a commitment to make a higher education place available to all those who were suitably qualified. This initiated a major expansion of higher education by recommending the establishment of polytechnics, based upon the premise that a key aim of higher education should be to develop employment-related skills.

Yet, five years later, the Committee on Manpower Resources for Science and Technology (1968) reported a continuing difficulty with attracting well-qualified and skilled graduates into science, technology and engineering in the United Kingdom. The Robbins Report had kick-started a rise in the percentage of under-21 students engaged in higher education, which increased from around 5 per cent to nearly 15 per cent by 1970 (Bathmaker, 2003), but expansion then levelled off until the late 1980s. In 1988 another rapid rise in student numbers was recorded, largely within polytechnics and colleges of higher education, following the Education Reform Act (DES, 1988) which created a new funding body for polytechnics and higher education colleges away from local authority control. This rise was further fuelled in 1992 when the two-sector, or binary, system was abolished by the Further and Higher Education Act (DES, 1992), allowing polytechnics to declare themselves universities.

In 1997, the National Committee of Inquiry into Higher Education chaired by Sir Ron Dearing highlighted the importance of developing higher education level qualifications as part of a strategy for increasing participation in higher education, in effect giving the government a green light to pursue its growing commitment to widening access and participation and to explore higher education expansion. Dearing expected that much of this expansion would be at 'sub-degree level' – an early indication of the role that Foundation Degrees came to have in the expansion of higher education (and this is explored more fully in the next section of this chapter). The 'Future of Higher Education' report (DfES, 2003) clarified a Labour government target of 50 per cent participation within higher education by 2010 for the 18–30 age group, although recent statistics show that the proportion of young adults entering higher education has stalled (DIUS, 2008). Nevertheless, the Higher Education Funding Council for England's (HEFCE) strategic plan states that 'widening access and increasing participation remains a crucial part of our mission' (HEFCE, 2009, p. 6).

Within the context of higher education expansion, the government at the time identified Foundation Degree provision as having a key part to play in meeting widening participation targets and providing appropriately skilled employees for the nation's workforce:

> We want to see expansion in two-year, work-focused Foundation Degrees; and in mature students in the workforce developing their skills. As we do this, we will maintain the quality standards required for access to university, both safeguarding the standards of traditional honours degrees and promoting a step-change in the quality and reputation of work-focused courses. (DfES, 2003, para 5.10)

The role identified here for Foundation Degrees in terms of providing the means to promote a proposed 'step-change' in the quality of work-focused courses within higher education is an aspect not to be overlooked. Alongside the expansion of higher education, arising from a desire to engineer social and economic equality for individuals as well as securing national economic prosperity, there were significant developments within the sphere of vocational education and the development of work-based higher education courses, and these are considered next.

Work-based higher education and the 'new vocationalism'

'New vocationalism' began in schools and colleges and has a specific history that runs parallel to the story of expansion outlined in the earlier section. During the 1970s, there was increasing dissatisfaction on the part of the government and employers with the quality of both school leavers and university graduates who appeared to be ill-equipped to contribute to a technologically advancing society. During what became known as the 'Great Debate' at Ruskin College in 1976, James Callaghan reported the concerns expressed to him during his tour of Britain, carried out over the first few months of his term as prime minister. As well as complaints from industry that school leavers were not equipped to enter the world of work, Callaghan also conveyed concern that graduates in subjects such as mathematics, science and technology had no desire to join industry. Therefore, it seemed that a dual approach to the future development of vocational education was needed – one that focused not only upon school leavers, but also upon higher education graduates.

During the 1970s and 1980s, many responses to the skills shortage among school leavers focused upon job-specific training that served to underline the divisions and distinctions between vocational and academic studies by narrowly defining skills and competencies (Farley, 1985; Boreham, 2002; Hager and Hyland, 2003). This drive comprised initiatives such as Youth Training Schemes (YTS), National Vocational Qualifications (NVQs) and others. The pathway for vocational qualifications became highly competence-based and was even viewed as devaluing vocational learning by some (Boreham, 2002; Hyland, 2006). Crucially, as there developed a growing recognition of the need to move away from the narrowness of pure vocational qualifications to have transferable skills and knowledge, and to draw back from the polarization of vocational and academic learning, the 'new vocationalism' was born within schools (Dale, 1985; Pollard et al., 1988). Initially, this was in the form of the Technical and Vocational Education Initiative (TVEI): rather than focusing exclusively upon skills training, the new vocationalism was more about enabling 'occupational versatility and personal adjustment' (Dale, 1985, p. 7), to bridge the gap between meeting the needs of industry and supporting individual pupils in fully realizing their potential.

Within the post-compulsory sector, the phrase 'the new vocationalism' was used to describe courses which sought to provide higher-level applicable knowledge and skills (Symes and McIntyre, 2000; Hager and Hyland, 2003). Of growing importance at this time was the need for traditional understandings of higher education to be reinterpreted and reconstructed within the context of the working world, while at the same time trying not to perpetuate the academic-vocational divide. In this respect, the 'Choosing to change' report (Higher Education Quality Council, 1994) recommended qualifications at the Higher Education Intermediate level, which combined vocational relevance and the potential for further progression within the higher education framework, as well as enhanced employment opportunities. In 1997, the 'Dearing' report highlighted the role that higher education level qualifications could play as part of a strategy for increasing participation. This was followed by two reports of the National Skills Task Force (DfEE, 1998; 1999), the second of which 'Delivering skills for all' (DfEE, 1999) recommended exploring a new system of two-year associate degrees in vocational subjects to support progression from Level 3 qualifications such as National Vocational Qualifications (NVQs). In addition, organizations such as the Council for Industry and Higher Education (established in 1986), the Centre for Education and Industry (established in 1988) and more recently, enterprise and employability-focused Centres of Excellence for Teaching and Learning (CETLS) plus initiatives such as the Higher Education Innovation Fund (HEIF), have spawned a range of higher education-based activities linked to graduate enterprise and employability.

Alongside the reappraisal of vocational training and education from a narrow to a broader conception within 'the new vocationalism', a growing feature of educational and political discourse was reference to the 'knowledge-based economy'. This appears in the foreword to the Foundation Degrees consultation document (DfEE, 2000) and underlines the political endorsement of a growing societal expectation that specialist knowledge was fast becoming the key currency for economic growth and success. The discourse surrounding the knowledge-based economy (an economy where knowledge has become a commodity to be produced, distributed and used) can be construed as challenging higher education as the central producer of knowledge, although commentators assert that the university has long held a central part in the production of knowledge and that this can, and should, continue (Symes and McIntyre, 2000; Delanty, 2001). What is clear, though, is that different forms of knowledge have gained legitimacy in a range of academic, work-based, professional and personal contexts (Eraut, 1994; Gibbons et al., 1994; Symes and McIntyre, 2000; Boud and Solomon, 2001; Delanty, 2001) underlining a growing deconstruction of traditional knowledge and institutional boundaries. This development appears to be inevitable within the context of the 'knowledge economy' and signifies a change in perception of what a university education may entail.

The developments outlined above created a climate in which it was no longer acceptable to polarize academic and vocational skills or knowledge and understanding. Instead, the new vocationalism promoted a more integrated approach both to fulfil widening access and participation targets for higher education and to provide education and training for employment within a rapidly changing and globalized economy, struggling with skills shortages among the workforce. In addition, the deconstruction of traditional knowledge and institutional boundaries was leading to the development of higher education courses that sought to apply knowledge in a range of contexts, not just act as transmitters of abstract knowledge (Gibbons et al., 1994). To this effect, work-based learning was seen as the 'new frontier' (Raelin, 2000), as 'a new higher education' (Boud and Solomon, 2001) and as 'new practices for new times' (Boud et al., 2001). The nature and scope of work-based learning is discussed more fully in Chapter 2.

In summary, Foundation Degrees developed from a desire to meet employer needs in addressing skills and knowledge shortages at the same time as providing a means for entry to and progression through the higher education framework, thus contributing to widening access and participation. They have developed within the context of a continuing reappraisal of what constitutes vocational education and training, as well as what constitutes valid 'knowledge' within the academy. Linking these debates has been the common thread of an emerging 'new vocationalism', which has emphasized the need to reinterpret and reconstruct traditional understandings of higher education within the context of today's working world (Barnett, 2000), and to embrace work-based learning in higher education contexts. Foundation Degrees have emerged as a new form of work-based learning within higher education, with specific features that give the degree its uniqueness. The uniqueness of the degree will be explored next.

Foundation Degrees: policy and practice

The integration of academic study and work is fundamental to the Foundation Degree model, as emphasized by the Quality Assurance Agency (QAA) Benchmark for Foundation Degrees which expects the programmes of study to be 'underpinned by work-based learning' (QAA, 2010, p. 7) and the DfES, who state explicitly that 'a Foundation Degree is a vocational higher education qualification which combines academic study with work-based learning and experience' (DfES, 2004, p. 3). Those studying for Foundation Degrees may be seeking to enter a profession, or may have worked within a profession for a while and the qualification is designed to provide opportunities for individuals to engage in lifelong learning (QAA, 2010). The QAA requires that opportunities for progression from Foundation Degrees are identified within individual institutions, with courses normally linked to a programme leading to an honours degree (QAA, 2010).

Foundation Degrees were first announced in February 2000 by the then Secretary of State for Education, David Blunkett, in his 'Modernising higher education – facing the global challenge' speech (DfES, 2000). The Foundation Degrees consultation document (DfEE, 2000) identified the qualifications framework offered by the community college model in the United States as a format upon which Foundation Degrees were to be based. This model provides two-year courses focused on specialist technical and professional skills, closely aligned to employer needs and with core skills seen as central for success. A major theme in the United States was to increase participation in post-secondary education, to create a more inclusive society. The same targets are now associated with Foundation Degrees in England and Wales as higher education expands to include those previously disenfranchised by higher education. In particular, the Foundation Degree qualification benchmark states explicitly that Foundation Degrees are designed 'to address shortages in particular skills [and] to contribute to widening participation and lifelong learning' (QAA, 2010, p. 1).

The first Foundation Degree courses started pilot schemes in September 2001 and a target of 100,000 students was set for 2010

(Foundation Degree Task Force, 2004). HEFCE (2010) reported that 99,475 students were registered on Foundation Degree programmes at higher education institutions (HEIs) and further education colleges (FECs) in 2009–2010, just 525 short of the target set. The chairman of the Foundation Degree Task Force, Professor Leslie Wagner, signified the perceived potential that Foundation Degrees have for moving vocational education on in the twenty-first century, yet also acknowledged the difficulties faced in fully integrating Foundation Degrees within the qualifications framework and in supporting effective and appropriate partnerships for work-based learning:

> Foundation Degrees represent both an opportunity and a challenge. The opportunity is to create a new type of provision meeting the need for a high quality, intermediate, vocational higher education qualification. The challenge is to produce it through partnership, developing effective work-based learning and integration with the existing qualification system. (Foundation Degree Task Force, 2004, p. 3)

The Task Force identified, then, an opportunity for Foundation Degrees to represent a 'new type of provision' – a distinctive higher-level, work-based, vocational qualification. In this respect, QAA (2010) makes it clear that the distinctiveness of the Foundation Degree is dependent not only upon its work-based nature, but also upon the integration of certain characteristics, which are employer involvement, accessibility, articulation and progression, flexibility and partnership. Many of these characteristics are recognizable in other programmes, for example in the Higher National Diploma (HND) and vocational degree courses, but it is 'their clear and planned integration within a single award, underpinned by work-based learning that makes the award very distinctive' (QAA, 2010, p. 7). Crucially, it is the distinctiveness of these integrated features that may have some impact upon student learning, so these features are considered next, in turn.

Employer involvement

A driving force behind the introduction of Foundation Degrees was a demand from employers for a higher level of skills among the workforce (Higher Education Quality Council, 1994; DfEE, 1998; DfEE, 1999;

Leitch, 2006). Foundation Degrees are therefore intended to give students the specific knowledge, understanding and skills that employers need. This implies employer involvement in the design of programmes and in monitoring the 'currency' of knowledge, skills and understanding that the programmes produce. However, the exact nature of employer involvement has not been specifically defined by policy makers, resulting in varied practice across the Foundation Degree sector. Edmond (2004) suggests that, within the practice of Foundation Degree delivery, and within relevant documentation, there is a perceived conflict between the desire to prioritize the needs of employers and ambiguous discourse regarding the role of employers that does not clarify their needs or specify their role. In my own experience as a Foundation Degree programme leader and as an external examiner, I have observed that employer involvement could be as minimal as the provision of an environment in which the Foundation Degree student can work (as an employee or a volunteer) or as much as the provision of financial support and involvement in course design and assessment. Furthermore, the inherent difficulty involved in engaging employers has become an all too familiar theme within Foundation Degree delivery. For example, work by Foskett (2003) emphasizes the difficulties and barriers to curriculum change within the context of partnership working, citing cultural disparities between academic institution and workplace as a particular challenge when attempting to meet a variety of expectations from stakeholders.

The Foundation Degree Task Force, charged with advising the government on future implementation strategy for Foundation Degrees, was asked to consider how best to secure employer involvement, with the resulting report describing employer involvement as 'at the heart of what makes the Foundation Degree distinctive' (Foundation Degree Task Force, 2004, p. 28). The Task Force suggested three strands of employer involvement, which form a useful framework around which to consider progress in this area: involvement in development and design; delivery and assessment; supporting students and employing Foundation Degree graduates, with a view to giving credibility to the Foundation Degree qualification.

In relation to development and design, the Leitch Report (Leitch, 2006) – tasked with considering the United Kingdom's long-term skills needs – has explicitly championed the further development of work-based courses that not only respond to employer demand, but which also attract financial investment from the employer as key stakeholder. Such investment is expected to cover all levels of work-based education and training from apprenticeships for school leavers, to the development of more intermediate-level degree courses (such as Foundation Degrees) for adults to support the development of higher-level skills. The direction given by Leitch reflects the QAA Foundation Degree qualification benchmark (2010) which explicitly states the expectation that employers will be involved in the design and review of Foundation Degrees. In this respect, Brennan (2004) cites the successful model of Foundation Degrees in Police Studies, for which employers have been fully involved in programme design, assessment and workplace support, thus incorporating all three strands of employer involvement, as suggested by the Task Force. However, this is perhaps an isolated success story, for a collection of case studies presented by Brennan and Gosling (2004) generally present a much poorer picture in terms of employer engagement:

> Many of the authors refer to a lack of understanding by employers of what is expected of them and confess to being uncertain about the nature and status of the foundation degree qualification. In some cases real tensions have been reported between the emphasis on training and specialist skills demanded by employers and the academic requirements of degree level study. (Brennan and Gosling, 2004, p. 15)

However, if securing employer involvement in the development and design stages is a challenge in itself, retaining involvement in delivery and possibly in assessment – the second recommendation from the Foundation Degree Task Force (2004) – becomes the next hurdle. For example, Green (2006) was surprised to find instances where regular meetings between employers and course teams seemed very rare. The exchange of information seemed to be a cause for concern with some partnerships, and he found that:

> The experience of what was required of the employer/provider in respect of work-based learning opportunities seemed to be surrounded by vagueness in many cases. Few had received any kind of guidance from course staff about the kind of work the student might be expected to

> produce; the process for supervising the component; the role of mentoring (only existing in few cases); the process of giving feedback to students, and the role played by the providing organisation in the process.
> (Green, 2006, p. 30)

Furthermore, Duckworth (2006) described the difficulties in securing employer representation at university-based meetings designed to assure programme quality. Employers cited the following reasons for non-engagement: 'geographical constraints; time available, and timing of meetings to name but a few' (Duckworth, 2006, p. 47). Perhaps Green and Duckworth had uncovered more of the cultural disparities between academy and workplace found by Foskett (2003), or perhaps the ineffective relationship between employer and higher education institution was purely down to poor communication. Either way, the learning experience for the work-based student becomes a cause for concern when employers are not engaged effectively, with a real danger being that 'there is the temptation to dilute the vital work-based learning components in Foundation Degrees. This needs resisting' (Connor, 2005, p. 25).

Government discourse makes employer involvement in Foundation Degrees a requirement, but still does not clarify the extent to which involvement by a single employer may be required. For example, Green (2006) found different perspectives on the benefit of work-based components within the courses investigated. Students in employment experienced different levels of flexibility from their employers in terms of gaining additional work experience, often dependent upon the sector in which they were working. For example, service constraints within the Health and Social Care sector meant that students could not gain an insight into professional areas beyond their own work situation. For students who were responsible for securing a voluntary work placement, Green found that there were dangers inherent in the student's reliance upon the employer to provide worthwhile working and learning experiences for them. This resulted in situations where some students were not fully integrated into the organization and, in some cases, were involved in work that may have been inappropriate for the student to engage in.

Hulbert has suggested that, to avoid some of the problematic areas outlined above, employer engagement 'does need to be better understood and articulated as a longitudinal continuum of partnership' (Hulbert, 2007, p. 13). Such a partnership would involve employer and higher education institution collaboration not only with course design, but also profile-raising for the Foundation Degree through marketing (nationally and locally) to develop a shared understanding among the academic and work-based communities of the unique features of the Foundation Degree related to employer engagement. The continuum would then need to extend more explicitly to the employment of Foundation Degree graduates – the final part of the third strand to the Foundation Degree Task Force's recommendations.

Reflection point

How does your institution engage employers with Foundation Degree provision? More about employer engagement can be found in Chapters 4, 5 and 8.

Accessibility, articulation and progression

The political impetus behind the introduction of Foundation Degrees had the agenda of inclusion and access at its centre. The Foundation Degree benchmark states explicitly that 'Foundation Degrees are intended to increase access and widen participation into higher education' (QAA, 2010, p. 7). This could be interpreted as access related to both geographical proximity of an institution and to ease of access to the course by students with non-traditional qualifications (usually qualifications other than A levels). Therefore, Foundation Degrees are expected to be delivered locally, targeting local students, and may take account of experience as well as qualifications when assessing entry qualifications for the course. Additionally, many learners should be able to work full- or part-time, often as part of their Foundation Degree, or combine voluntary work relevant to the course with paid employment elsewhere, thus increasing accessibility in terms of financial support.

In addition, the benchmark states that 'Foundation Degrees are intended to make a valuable contribution to lifelong learning' (QAA,

2010, p. 8). In this respect, a further defining characteristic of the Foundation Degree is the prospect of progression within work and/ or to a suitable honours degree. This feature was emphasized at the consultation stage (DfEE, 2000) as an essential component of the new qualification. By situating the Foundation Degree as a Level 5 qualification in higher education, achievement at this level can provide progression opportunities to other higher education and/or professional qualifications. Therefore, there are built-in aspirational possibilities for Foundation Degree students in terms of progressing to honours degree study, which may open up further possibilities for future progression within the postgraduate qualifications framework. Thus, Foundation Degrees have the real potential to contribute to the widening participation agenda.

However, although access and progression policies for Foundation Degree students are designed to increase numbers of non-traditional entrants to higher education, support for such students goes far beyond just providing an opportunity to engage with higher education. Unless well supported, Foundation Degree students are in danger of not feeling well prepared for higher education study. In addition, previous negative experiences of educational systems (e.g. failure to achieve academic qualifications at school) may have imbued within the Foundation Degree student feelings of self-doubt, while the management of multiple roles as part-time student, employee and possibly even parent can mean that the experience of higher-level study is characterized by conflict and struggle. Nevertheless, key principles that underpin the design and delivery of Foundation Degrees in relation to flexibility and partnership have the potential to create learning environments that could mitigate difficulties for the Foundation Degree learner and it is these aspects of the Foundation Degree that are considered next.

Reflection point

What does access to and progression from Foundation Degrees look like in your institution?

More about access can be found in Chapter 3.

More about designing progression routes can be found in Chapter 4.

Flexibility and partnership

The notion of flexibility is applied broadly to Foundation Degrees to include the institution, the learner and the employer. Institutions are expected to recognize and respond to the needs of learners from a variety of backgrounds and with a range of qualifications and experience. In practice, this might mean flexible study patterns (e.g. full- and part-time, distance learning, evening and weekend learning, web-based learning etc.) (QAA, 2010). In addition, it might lead to keener attention being given to flexibility of teaching strategies, buoyed in higher education pedagogy circles in recent years by a greater understanding of how students learn, developed against a backdrop of moves to professionalize teaching in higher education. However, Challis (2005, p. 18) acknowledges that 'Flexibility in this context is a difficult issue to pin down', contending that flexible delivery is not just a matter of curriculum change, but that 'truly flexible provision is built around specific and identified needs of prospective learners on the programme'. True flexibility, then, demands a consideration of the learner and their needs – an approach that attempts to provide a learning experience that is relevant to the individual rather than expecting the individual to adapt to a fixed programme of study.

Flexible delivery is underlined in the Foundation Degree Task Force Report (2004) as an important factor for accessibility. This can mean a very different student experience for Foundation Degree students to that of 'conventional' students. However, the flexibility demanded of Foundation Degree delivery is now expected more widely within higher education, in the context of widening access initiatives. For example, the survey conducted by Osborne and Young (2006) of widening access initiatives across the United Kingdom described the range as including in-reach (developing new ways for potential students to access provision), out-reach (collaboration, partnership and raising awareness of the benefits of higher education to under-represented groups) and as also to do with 'transformations and adjustments to the structure, administrations and delivery of HE programmes' (Osborne and Young, 2006, p. 6) – in other words, concerned with more flexibility. Osborne and Young summarize the trend towards flexibility:

> Flexibility in the context of widening participation refers to both spatial and temporal matters, namely changes that allow students access to

education in locations and modes, and at times that, to at least a certain degree, are of individuals' rather than institutions' choosing. (Osborne and Young, 2006, p. 9)

Partnerships within Foundation Degrees may be made across a wide spectrum. For example, higher education and further education partnerships, employer and institution partnerships, partnership with other organizations such as sector skills councils, to name but a few. Partnerships with employers have already been identified (in the previous section) as a challenging area largely due to different expectations and cultural disparities on the part of the academic institution and the employer. Higher education and further education partnerships are also not without their challenges.

Reflection point

Are you fully aware of the extent of partnership working at your institution? How could these partnerships be used effectively to support Foundation Degree learners?

More about collaborative provision and partnership working can be found in Chapter 4.

Summary

Foundation Degrees possess the following key characteristics (QAA, 2010):

- employer involvement
- accessibility, articulation and progression
- flexibility and partnership.

If fully integrated, these characteristics have the potential to render the Foundation Degree programme a unique educational offering to those who previously would not have entered higher education. However, these characteristics present challenges to Foundation Degree design and delivery and to the quality of the Foundation Degree student experience. Throughout the rest of this book, each of these unique characteristics will be explored within the contexts of learner needs, course design, teaching strategies, e-learning and assessment.

References

Barnett, R. (2000), 'Foreword', in Symes, C. and McIntyre, J. (eds), *Working Knowledge: The New Vocationalism and Higher Education.* Buckingham, UK: SRHE/Open University Press, pp. ix–x.

Bathmaker, A. -M. (2003), 'The expansion of higher education: a consideration of control, funding and quality', in Bartlett, S. and Burton, D. (eds), *Education Studies: Essential Issues.* London: Sage, pp. 169–189.

Boreham, N. (2002), 'Work process knowledge, curriculum control and the work-based route to curriculum qualifications', *British Journal of Educational Studies*, 50 (2), 225–237.

Boud, D. and Solomon, N. (eds) (2001), *Work-Based Learning: A New Higher Education?* Buckingham, UK: SRHE/Open University Press.

Boud, D., Solomon, N. and Symes, C. (2001), 'New practices for new times', in Boud, D. and Solomon, N. (eds), *Work-Based Learning: A New Higher Education?* Buckingham, UK: SRHE/Open University Press, pp. 3–17.

Brennan, L. (2004), 'Making Foundation Degrees work: an introduction and overview', in Brennan, L. and Gosling, D. (eds), *Making Foundation Degrees Work.* London: SEEC, pp. 1–29.

Brennan, L. and Gosling, D. (eds) (2004), *Making Foundation Degrees Work.* London: SEEC.

Callaghan, J. (1976), The speech by Prime Minister James Callaghan at Ruskin College Oxford. Available online at: http://education.guardian.co.uk/thegreatdebate/story/0,,574645, 00.html (accessed 1 April 2008).

Challis, M. (2005), 'Challenging issues for Foundation Degree providers: flexible delivery', *Forward: The Foundation Degree Forward Journal*, 4, 18–21.

Committee on Higher Education (1963), *Report of the Committee on Higher Education (the Robbins Report).* London: HMSO.

Committee on Manpower Resources for Science and Technology (1968), *The Brain Drain: Report of the Working Group on Migration.* London: HMSO.

Connor, H. (2005), 'Employer engagement', *Forward: The Foundation Degree Forward Journal*, 4, 24–26.

Dale, R. (ed.) (1985), *Education, Training and Employment: Towards a New Vocationalism?* Oxford: Pergamon.

Dearing, R. (1997), *Higher Education in a Learning Society: The National Committee into Higher Education.* London: HMSO.

Delanty, G. (2001), *Challenging Knowledge: The University in the Knowledge Society.* Buckingham, UK: SRHE/Open University Press.

DES (1988), *Education Reform Act.* Available online at: www.legislation.gov.uk/ukpga/1988/40/ contents (accessed 14 March 2011).

— (1992), *Further and Higher Education Act*. Available online at: www.legislation.gov.uk/ ukpga/1992/13/contents (accessed 14 March 2011).

DfEE (1998), *First Report of the National Skills Task Force: Towards a National Skills Agenda*. London: DfEE.

— (1999), *Second Report of the National Skills Task Force: Delivering Skills for All*. London: DfEE.

— (2000), 'Foundation Degrees' – consultation paper. London: DfEE.

DfES (2000), *Modernising Higher Education – Facing the Global Challenge*. Available online at: www.cms1.gre.ac.uk/dfee/#speech (accessed 2 April 2008).

— (2003), *The Future of Higher Education*. Nottingham: DfES. Available online at: www.bis. gov.uk/assets/biscore/corporate/migratedd/publications/f/future_of_he.pdf (accessed 15 March 2011).

— (2004), *The Employer Guide to Foundation Degrees*. Nottingham: DfES.

DIUS (2008), *Participation Rates in Higher Education Academic Years 1999/2000–2006/2007 (Provisional)*. Available online at: www.education.gov.uk/rsgateway/DB/SFR/s000780/ dsfr02-2008.pdf (accessed 15 March 2011).

Duckworth, L. (2006), '"Recycling" Fd early years graduates: strategies for enhancing employer engagement through the training of mentors', *Forward: The Foundation Degree Forward Journal*, 9, 47–48.

Edmond, N. (2004), 'The Foundation Degree as evidence of a new higher education: a study of HE provision for teaching assistants', *Higher Education Review*, 36 (3), 33–53.

Eraut, M. (1994), *Developing Professional Knowledge and Competence*. London: RoutledgeFalmer.

Farley, M. (1985), 'Trends and structural changes in English vocational education', in Dale, R. (ed.) *Education, Training and Employment: Towards a New Vocationalism?* Oxford: Pergamon, pp. 73–94.

Foskett, R. (2003), 'Employer and needs-led curriculum planning in Higher Education: a cross-sector case study of foundation degree development'. Available online at: www. leeds.ac.uk/educol/documents/00003182.htm (accessed 12 January 2009).

Foundation Degree Task Force (2004), *Report to Ministers*. London: DfES.

Gibbons, M., Limoges, C., Nowotny, H., Schwartzman, S., Scott, P. and Trow, M. (1994), *The New Production of Knowledge*. London: Sage.

Green, C. (2006), 'The perceived benefit of work-based learning – capturing the views of students, staff and employers', *Forward: The Foundation Degree Forward Journal*, 9, 27–30.

Hager, P. and Hyland, T. (2003), 'Vocational education and training', in Blake, N., Smeyers, P., Smith, R. and Standish, P. (eds), *The Blackwell Guide to the Philosophy of Education*. Oxford: Blackwell, pp. 271–287.

HEFCE (2009), *Strategic Plan 2006–11*. London: HEFCE. Available online at: www.hefce. ac.uk/pubs/hefce/2009/09_21/09_21.pdf (accessed 15 March 2011).

— (2010), *Foundation Degrees: Key Statistics 2001–02 to 2009–10*. Available online at: www. hefce.ac.uk/pubs/hefce/2010/10_12 (accessed 21 October 2010).

HEQC (1994), *Choosing to Change: Extending Access, Choice and Mobility in Higher Education*. London: HEQC.

Hulbert, F. (2007), 'The Foundation Degree – nexus complexus', *Forward: The Foundation Degree Forward Journal*, 12, 12–15.

Hyland, T. (2006), 'Vocational education and training and the therapeutic turn', *Educational Studies*, 32 (3), 299–306.

Leitch, S. (2006), *Prosperity for All in the Global Economy – World Class Skills*. Available online at: www.hm-treasury.gov.uk/leitch (accessed 15 March 2011).

Osborne, M. and Young, D. (2006), *Flexibility and Widening Participation*. Bristol, UK: ESCalate.

Pollard, A., Purvis, J. and Walford, G. (eds) (1988), *Education, Training and the New Vocationalism: Experience and Policy*. Milton Keynes, UK: Open University Press.

QAA (2008), *The Framework for Higher Education Qualifications in England, Wales and Northern Ireland (FHEQ)*. Available online at: www.qaa.ac.uk/Publications/InformationAndGuidance/Documents/FHEQ08.pdf (accessed 30 August 2011).

— (2010), *Foundation Degree Qualification Benchmark*. Gloucester, UK: QAA.

Raelin, J. A. (2000), *Work-Based Learning: The New Frontier of Management Development*. New Jersey: Prentice Hall.

Symes, C. and McIntyre, J. (eds) (2000), *Working Knowledge: The New Vocationalism and Higher Education*. Buckingham, UK: SRHE/Open University Press.

2 Work-Based Learning

Claire Taylor

This chapter will:

- present definitions of work-based learning
- discuss and reflect upon 'socially situated learning' and 'experiential learning' as key characteristics of work-based learning
- explore the nature of knowledge in relation to work-based learning
- explore work-based learning in practice.

Introduction

It is important that tutors have a well-developed understanding of the nature of work-based learning to bring a robust intellectual rationale and fully thought through philosophical approach to Foundation Degree design and delivery. That is not to say that there is a 'one size fits all' view of what Foundation Degree work-based learning in higher education means and looks like. However, I would suggest that there are key areas that clearly relate to work-based learning pedagogy and to the Foundation Degree model in particular, that have engendered debate among the academic community and which are worthy of further exploration here, namely:

- how to define work-based learning in the higher education context
- the nature of work-based learning as social practice
- the role of experiential learning in the work-based context
- work-based learning and forms of knowledge.

Defining work-based learning

In Chapter 1, I suggested that the Foundation Degree – a work-based higher education qualification (QAA, 2010) that combines higher-level knowledge and understanding alongside vocational competence – would seem to be situated within the tradition of higher education work-based learning. However, even though Boud and Symes (2000, p. 15) stated at the turn of the millennium that 'work-based learning is [. . .] an idea whose time has come', defining work-based learning within the context of higher education is more problematic. Indeed, there are potential difficulties of interpretation when referring to work-based learning and what the term may mean, with the Foundation Degree Task Force Report (2004) noting that 'a variety of similar sounding terms are used to describe the work element of higher education programmes. This includes "work-oriented", "work-related", "work-focused", "work-placed", "work-based"' (2004, p. 20).

Boud et al. (2001) are clear that 'work-based learning is the term being used to describe a class of university programmes that bring together universities and work organizations to create new learning opportunities in the workplace' (2001, p. 4). The emphasis here is upon the workplace as providing a forum for learning, within a university (higher education) level programme, developed as a partnership between university and work. This is consonant with the Foundation Degree model where situational, work-based learning is a significant mechanism for learning and demands not only workplace support, but cross-sector partnerships between employers and institutions (Foskett, 2003; Foundation Degree Task Force, 2004; QAA, 2010).

However, others consider the scope of learning at work to also include unintentional, informal learning through workplace socialization (Lohman, 2000; Guile and Young, 2001; Billett, 2002a, 2002b; Dirkx et al., 2002). In this respect, Billet (2002a, 2002b) has outlined how informal workplace learning allows individuals to construct meaning from their experiences, while Lohman (2000, p. 84) has extended the scope of informal work-based learning to include 'activities initiated by people in work settings that result in the development of their professional skills and knowledge', thus suggesting that work-based learning may occur along a planned–unplanned continuum. Dirkx et al. (2002) even suggest a hybrid of informal and formal learning – structured activities used to study and learn from specific aspects of work, based upon 'action learning' (also described by Raelin, 2000; McGill and Beaty, 2001; McGill and Brockbank, 2004).

Raelin (2000) brings a further dimension to the discussion by suggesting that engaging in work-based learning is not just about collecting knowledge and a set of skills, rather it arises from shared action and problem solving, thus underlining the social mode of learning in the workplace. This view is shared by Beaney (2005) who brings many of these points together by emphasizing that work-based learning is situational and socially shaped.

Reflection point

How do you and your teaching team define work-based learning?

Are there variations of interpretation between tutors or subject areas?

Is it important that a common definition is shared between the team, or could such variations enhance your Foundation Degree programmes?

Work-based learning as social practice

Essentially, it is clear from the discussion around work-based learning definitions, discussed in the previous section, that work-based learning is situational and socially shaped (Lohman, 2000; Raelin 2000; Guile and Young, 2001; Billett, 2002a, 2002b; Dirkx et al., 2002; Beaney, 2005) and to explore this idea further the work of Lave and Wenger (1991) and Wenger (1998, 2002), is explored next.

In the early 1990s, Lave and Wenger's (1991) anthrop
learning as part of social activity was seen as a move a
tional' views of learning and learners, as promoted by c
such as Piaget (1953) and Gagné (1985). Such theor
part of the learner in actively processing responses, through ...
the mind. In addition, fundamental to the cognitive theorists' premise is
the idea that learning 'is controlled by the inherent structure of knowledge itself' (Rogers, 2002, p. 10) – a view that lends itself to hierarchical
models of learning such as those developed by Bloom et al. (1956) and
Gagné (1985). In contrast, Lave and Wenger (1991) contend that learning is not something undertaken individually and in isolation, but is
seen as participation in the social world. They view social engagement,
rather than cognitive processes, as the key to effective learning and this
has clear relevance for work-based learning.

Lave and Wenger see situated learning as a gradual and growing
engagement, beginning as a novice practitioner engaging in 'legitimate
peripheral participation' (Lave and Wenger, 1991) and developing along
a continuum to becoming a full participant in a 'community of practice'.
In engaging in 'legitimate peripheral participation', the learner 'partici-
pates in the actual practice of an expert' (Hanks, 1991, p. 14) and in
this respect is engaged in activity that appears credible and worthwhile
to experts. However, the participation is initially limited; it is purpose-
fully peripheral to allow development along the continuum to full,
non-peripheral participation. The notion of participation itself is also a
crucial idea for Lave and Wenger, where the focus is on the community
rather than on the individual. In this respect, learning takes place within
a framework of participation, rather than within an individual mind,
enabling learning to be distributed among those participating.

However, in considering their framework, it is important not to narrow Lave and Wenger's concept of a 'community of practice' (Lave and
Wenger, 1991; Wenger, 1998), rather 'a community of practice is a set of
relations among persons, activity, and world, over time and in relation
with other tangential and overlapping communities of practice' (Lave
and Wenger, 1991, p. 98). Thus, the community of practice is not merely
a shared working space or physical environment. Instead it is relational
and encompasses active engagement with the world. Therefore, when
applied to the context of work-based learning, situated learning within

a community of practice which facilitates 'legitimate peripheral partici-pation' necessitates shared enterprise and an overt acknowledgement of the importance of relationships within the workplace for learning to happen effectively.

So, the relevance to work-based learning is clear – Lave and Wenger's work champions learning in the workplace community and gives us a potentially useful lens through which to view Foundation Degree learning. However, as with any approach, using Lave and Wenger's work as a means of understanding learning in the workplace has its strengths and weaknesses (Tennant, 2000; Dirkx et al., 2002; Fuller et al., 2005). For example, Fuller et al. acknowledge that the notion of 'legitimate peripheral participation' 'sheds considerable light on the processes involved when people newly enter a community' (Fuller et al., 2005, p. 65), but argue that the notion does not cater for those who continue to learn in the workplace having attained full member-ship of a team or department.

The inflexibility of Lave and Wenger's model is highlighted further when mapped to the Foundation Degree learner's experience. Lave and Wenger assume a model of 'novice practitioner' moving to experienced, or knowledgeable, practitioner. However, within Foundation Degree study, students are not always coming to the workplace as new members. Some with positions of responsibility or with many years of experience within the workplace are perceived as already established and integrated members of the community of practice. This renders the application of Lave and Wenger's continuum model of moving from novice to fully fledged practitioner within a stable, cohesive community of practice less than straightforward.

Nevertheless, many acknowledge that Lave and Wenger's work provides an invaluable starting point for developing a work-based learning pedagogy, particularly when considered alongside cognitive learning theory. For example, Billett (2002a, 2002b, 2002c) has devel-oped the model further to incorporate the relationship between the social and cognitive elements of learning in the workplace and also to incorporate guided learning within a work-based learning peda-gogy. For Billett, the notion of participation is 'a product of the evolv-ing social practice of the workplace, which is historically, culturally and situationally constructed, and the socially constructed personal history of the individual' (Billett, 2002c, p. 466). Billett acknowledges that learning in the workplace is multidimensional, combining learning as socially situated practice with the individual learner's cognitive framework and acknowledging the part that personal history plays in how individuals choose to engage in the workplace. Similarly, Dirkx et al. (2002) view as important the cognitive framework that the learner brings to the context of learning: 'what learners come to know and understand through the process of learning reflects who they are as persons and how they are making sense of their experiences in the workplace' (Dirkx et al., 2002, p. 6). Thus, social interaction, the learner's sense of self and personal experience play their part when learning within the workplace.

Case study: legitimate participation in practice

Lave and Wenger's (1991) work around situated learning and communities of practice describes the novice in the workplace developing to becoming a 'fully-fledged' worker. Although for some work-based Foundation Degree students this model is not wholly appropriate, as they already have considerable workplace experience, what does seem to be important is the extent to which work-based learners are allowed to extend their workplace experience.

For example, Kim studied for an education-related Foundation Degree, based in a primary school. During an average week she worked with five different teachers across different classes engaging with a mixture of groups and whole-class activities. In so doing, she was exposed to the routines and teaching practices of a range of colleagues within the school. Kim was given the opportunity by her employers to engage in different social learning activities through her differing roles within the workplace, thus 'extending' her participation and giving a variety of rich work-based contexts within which to situate her learning.

However, on the same Foundation Degree, Jo seemed to experience restricted participation within the workplace. This was due to lack of interest from colleagues, poor mentoring provision and 'political manoeuvring' between some staff members upon the arrival of a new head teacher which led to workplace conflict and the marginalization of the practical support available to Jo as a work-based learner. For Jo, the relationships between colleagues (teachers, teaching assistants, head teacher) became a sociocultural factor that restricted her participation in workplace practices and impacted upon the learning potential of the workplace.

Later chapters will address many of the issues that, if acted upon, may have assured a more positive workplace experience for Jo, but it is worth remembering that the Foundation Degree model brings an extra layer of pedagogical complexity through the dimension of work-based learning.

Experiential learning

Beaney (2005) highlights the importance of viewing work-based learning as a subset of experiential learning: 'It is the experience of work and how it is worked upon by appropriate abstract learning and reflection that makes work-based learning such a potentially powerful pedagogy' (Beaney, 2005, p. 6).

John Dewey's classic text 'Experience and Education' (1938) contains extensive observations about the connections between life (including work) experiences and learning. He wrote extensively about the educational value of integrating experience, learning and reflection upon it (Dewey 1938, 1966). He believed that all genuine education was the product of experience but was very clear that two key principles had to be present. First, that experiences that lead to learning are never isolated events – instead they build upon what has come before and depend upon the learner reflecting upon connecting present and past experiences to enlarge meaning. Secondly, the experience has to involve interaction between the learner and their environment – in other words, first-hand experience is vital.

Learner voice

Work-based Foundation Degree students recognize that having space to reflect and make valuable connections between theory and practice is a key component of their learning:

'In a workplace setting there's very little time for reflection . . . this course makes you find time and I think that's a good thing' Foundation Degree student Year 2.

'When you go back into your workplace the next day you think, "oh I know why that's happening."' (Foundation Degree student Year 2)

However, despite a broad consensus regarding the value of learning through experience and through processes of reflection, different commentators offer broad interpretations as to what constitutes experiential learning. Kolb (1984), for example, defines experience as involving action – or learning by doing. Kolb's learning cycle pinpoints four crucial stages that have to be travelled through for learning to happen: concrete experience (involving oneself in new experiences), reflective observation (observational and reflective skills – viewing the experiences from different perspectives), abstract conceptualization (analytically creating new concepts) and active experimentation (problem solving – using the new ideas or concepts). What is important in Kolb's model is the idea of progression in learning, coupled with the need to recycle the cycle, so that reflection, learning and action continue. However, Kolb's model does not take into account the learners' situation, nor their personal biographies. Therefore, it could be viewed as at odds, on the one hand, with the notion of learning as social practice (Lave and Wenger, 1991; Wenger, 1998, 2002) and, on the other, with the view of workplace pedagogic practice espoused by Billett (2002a, 2002b, 2002c) which incorporates an individual's personal history as discussed earlier. Essentially, the model seems to operate in a de-contextualized vacuum (apart from the immediate experience being engaged in), with the danger that the nature of learning becomes oversimplified. This view is reiterated by Moon who states that:

> Learning and the role of reflection in learning do not seem to be as tidy as the experiential learning cycle suggests. Even a simple application in a practical situation will indicate that, in reality, the process is 'messy', with stages re-cycling and interweaving as meaning is created and recreated. (Moon, 1999, p. 35)

Despite such difficulties, though, the common thread linking core elements of theorization related to experiential learning is the place of reflection and it is Schön, author of *The Reflective Practitioner* (1983), who attempted to elaborate and categorize the process of reflection through the models of reflection in and on action. This is a thread of inquiry relevant to learning within the workplace because Schön developed his ideas in the context of reflection in professional practice (Schön, 1983, 1987).

Schön's reflection-on-action happens after action and involves reflecting upon the action just taken. In this respect, it seems similar to the reflection identified by Kolb (1984) which occurs as part of a learning cycle that then leads to further action. Indeed, Moon suggests that 'Schön's notion of reflection-on-action is encompassed in Kolb's experiential learning cycle as the processing of experience' (Moon, 1999, p. 51). However, Schön (1983) claims that reflection-in-action is a significant characteristic of professional working and learning. This type of reflection occurs at the time of the action and forms a response to unexpected events as they unfold. Furthermore, in his consideration of how to educate the reflective practitioner, Schön (1987) highlights the role of the practitioner community in supporting the development of reflective practice from conscious reflection through to more intuitive reflection-in-action. This reflects the notion of learning as social practice, discussed previously in the context of communities of practice (Lave and Wenger, 1991; Wenger, 1998).

However, other commentators are not convinced by Schön's claims regarding reflection-in-action. For example, Eraut (1994), in analysing Schön's work, suggests that a focus on the 'reflective' element is unhelpful. Rather, Eraut contends that Schön is exploring metacognition in the context of professional knowledge. In addition, Moon (1999) suggests that the imprecise ways in which Schön uses the terms reflection-on-action and reflection-in-action does not support his claims for unique categories of reflection, particularly as reflection-on-action seems no different to the role of reflection within experiential learning. Nevertheless, Schön's work has inspired debate around the role of reflection in professional practice and also around the relationship between theory and practice within professional practice which is of relevance for a work-based course such as the Foundation Degree.

Reflection point

Search the internet for material related to 'reflective cycle'. You will probably be presented with a variety of models, images and descriptions, including Kolb's work (1984), described earlier. Consider:

How does your understanding of learning in the workplace fit with any one of these models?

Could you adapt one of these or develop your own model that reflects reflective learning in the workplace for use with your teaching team, or with students?

Work-based learning and forms of knowledge

Chapter 1 outlined significant changes that have occurred within the UK higher education landscape since the 1960s. They include the expansion of higher education and a political desire to reconstruct traditional understandings of higher education within the context of the working world. A consequence of such change has been the gradual deconstruction of traditional knowledge and institutional boundaries and this has been a key factor in the acceptance of work-based learning as a valid pedagogy.

In a seminal work (reappraising the nature of knowledge) Lyotard et al. (1984) suggest that knowledge has moved from being an abstract notion and the exclusive privilege of the intellectual elite, to becoming a fragmented commodity, relevant to specific settings and situations. As well as the nature of knowledge, sites of knowledge production have also shifted (Delanty, 2001). More specifically, for a work-based higher education course the workplace becomes a potential site of knowledge production, alongside the university (Tennant, 2000; Boud, 2001). However, the kinds of knowledge generated by the workplace and academic institution may be very different and an understanding of the differences is an important thread in developing an appreciation of work-based learning.

Gibbons et al. (1994) describe two kinds of knowledge production, calling them modes one and two. The features are summarized in Table 2.1.

Table 2.1 Mode one and mode two knowledge

Mode one knowledge	Mode two knowledge
Academic context	Produced in the context of application
Disciplinary knowledge	Transdisciplinary knowledge
Homogenous characteristics	Heterogeneous characteristics
Hierarchical knowledge	Transient
Produced inside 'traditional universities'	More socially accountable
	More reflexive
	Increasingly produced outside 'traditional' university' settings

Transdisciplinarity and applied knowledge are key characteristics of the mode two list, which appear to fit with the ideas discussed previously in relation to the situational and socially shaped nature of learning in the workplace (Raelin, 2000; Beaney, 2005). For example, knowledge produced through learning within a community of practice where groups of people share a common concern and grow together in their learning as they interact with one another (Lave and Wenger, 1991; Wenger, 1998) mirrors the notion of developing knowledge in the context of a particular application (the first aspect of mode two knowledge in Table 2.1).

In addition, the situatedness of workplace learning means that knowledge is specific to the workplace context and develops interactively and cumulatively in that context, rather than being derived from an academically contextualized theoretical solution. Furthermore, the cross-disciplinary, transient nature of such knowledge demands from the learner a reflexive approach, which parallels the reflection upon action that must be taken when engaging in any experiential learning (Schön, 1983; Kolb, 1984).

However, although mode two knowledge appears to fit well with work-based learning, Boud (2001) makes it clear that mode one knowledge is not rendered unnecessary, rather that it may be 'subordinated to other, more pressing agendas' (Boud, 2001, p. 37). So, for the work-based learner engaged in a Foundation Degree programme, aspects of mode one knowledge are clearly relevant for a course that demands collaboration between academic institution and workplace, but knowledge generated within the workplace (mode two knowledge) also holds legitimacy. Boud observes that a key challenge of the work-based learning curriculum is the extent to which the two modes of knowledge are reconciled, to design a curriculum that is both accessible and relevant for the work-based learner.

In addition, Eraut's work on theories of professional expertise and the development of a map of professional knowledge are particularly relevant for work-based learning and especially for specific sectors such as education. Eraut (1994) considers three types of knowledge – propositional, personal and process –and they are summarized in Table 2.2.

When related to the model developed by Gibbons et al. (1994), Eraut's 'propositional' type of knowledge most closely resembles

Table 2.2 Propositional, personal and process knowledge

Type of knowledge	Key characteristics
Propositional	Most traditional basis of teaching in Higher Education
	Discipline-based
	Theory
	Concepts
Personal	Based upon the impressions, experience and encounters of everyday life
	Some discrete experiences develop meaning when they are reflected upon
Process	Uses propositional knowledge
	Is about 'knowing how' – metaprocesses, skilled behaviour, deliberative processes

Gibbons et al.'s mode one knowledge. Eraut's 'personal' knowledge refers to the contribution that a learner's personal history makes to the situated learning experience. Eraut suggests that personal knowledge gains validity through the development of higher-level skills of reflection within the workplace, thus demonstrating affinity with the necessity of incorporating reflection within a work-based pedagogy to draw meaning from experience. Indeed, I would suggest that it is only through reflective practice in the workplace that students are able to make meaning of propositional knowledge, thus process knowledge sums up a key aspect of work-based learning pedagogy very well. For the Foundation Degree, therefore, the bringing together of professional and practical knowledge with subject-based, academic knowledge can result in a course that, if care is not taken, pulls in two directions. The challenge, then, is the integration of the two strands without compromising either type of knowledge brought to the course by student, workplace or institution.

Reflection point

Does your Foundation Degree successfully bring together professional, practical, subject-based and academic knowledge to create a vocationally orientated, yet academically robust, student experience?

Does your Foundation Degree teaching team privilege certain types of knowledge within the course, or are all aspects given equal and credible treatment?

Work-based learning in practice

Just as there are no shared or standard definitions regarding work-based learning in higher education, so there are also no standard forms of what work-based learning looks like in practice. With this in mind, achieving a good work-based learning experience will need to take account of the following factors:

- what is being delivered
- when it is being delivered
- where it is being delivered
- how it is being delivered.

These issues are covered in more depth later on in this book, but it is worth considering some brief examples here in the context of the earlier discussions in this chapter around the nature of work-based learning.

For example, the content of what is delivered in a Foundation Degree through work-based learning will be inextricably linked to the professional workplace context in which the course is situated. Furthermore, a wide range of approaches to how work-based learning is delivered will be seen across different Foundation Degrees, dependent on how course design, development and delivery is shared between different partners (such as the FEC, HEI, professional body or workplace itself) and will also be reflective of the status of the learner as full-time or part-time student and/or employee. In practice, work-based learning may be delivered as core modules, within placement contexts, as simulations or live projects, as a range of work-related activities, or as real work projects. Differences of approach are to be welcomed in terms of creating flexible opportunities for learners, but it is also important to be cognizant of providing a comparable, relevant and valuable work-based learning experience for all students. These and many other issues related to the delivery of work-based Foundation Degrees are discussed at length in subsequent chapters.

Summary

This chapter has attempted to give some 'food for thought' for those involved in the design and delivery of Foundation Degree tutors, in relation to understanding the nature of work-based learning. As well as considering how work-based learning may be defined, the chapter has also considered the nature of work-based learning as social practice, the role of experiential learning (and by implication, reflection) in the work-based context and forms of knowledge in relation to work-based learning. By engaging with these ideas and theoretical frameworks, all those involved in Foundation Degree teaching and learning should be well placed to develop approaches and perspectives firmly founded upon appropriate conceptual frameworks.

References

Beaney, P. (2005), 'All in a day's work? Unravelling the conceptual tangles around work-based learning and Foundation Degrees', *Forward: The Foundation Degree Forward Journal*, 4, 4–8.

Billett, S. (2002a), 'Workplace learning as co-participation', Paper presented at the Annual Meeting of the American Educational Research Association (New Orleans, LA, 1–5 April 2002).

— (2002b), 'Toward a workplace pedagogy: guidance, participation and engagement', *Adult Education Quarterly*, 53 (1), 27–43.

— (2002c), 'Workplace pedagogic practices: co-participation and learning', *British Journal of Educational Studies*, 50 (4), 457–481.

Bloom, B. S., Krathwohl, D. R., Engelhart, M. D., Furst, E. J. and Hill, W. H. (1956), *Taxonomy of Educational Objectives: Cognitive Domain*. London: Longman.

Boud, D. (2001), 'Knowledge at work: issues of learning', in Boud, D. and Solomon, N. (eds), *Work-Based Learning: A New Higher Education?* Buckingham, UK: SRHE /Open University Press, pp. 34–43.

Boud, D. and Solomon, N. (eds) (2001), *Work-Based Learning: A New Higher Education?* Buckingham, UK: SRHE/Open University Press.

Boud, D. and Symes, C. (2000), 'Learning for real: work-based education in universities', in Symes, C. and McIntyre, J. (eds), *Working Knowledge: The New Vocationalism and Higher Education*. Buckingham, UK: SRHE/Open University Press, pp. 14–29.

Boud, D., Solomon, N. and Symes, C. (2001), 'New practices for new times', in Boud, D. and Solomon, N. (eds), *Work-Based Learning: A New Higher Education?* Buckingham, UK: SRHE/Open University Press, pp. 3–17.

Delanty, G. (2001), *Challenging Knowledge: The University in the Knowledge Society*. Buckingham, UK: SRHE/Open University Press.

Dewey, J. (1938), *Experience and Education*. New York: Macmillan.

— (1966), *Selected Educational Writings*. London: Heinemann.

Dirkx, J. M., Swanson R. A., Watkins K. E. and Cseh, M. (2002), 'Design, demand, development and desire: a symposium on the discourses of workplace learning', Innovative session. Academy of Human Resource Development (AHRD) Conference Proceedings (Honolulu, Hawaii, 27 February–3 March 2002).

Eraut, M. (1994), *Developing Professional Knowledge and Competence*. London: RoutledgeFalmer.

Foskett, R. (2003), 'Employer and needs-led curriculum planning in higher education: a cross-sector case study of foundation degree development'. Available online at: www.leeds.ac.uk/educol/documents/00003182.htm (accessed 12 January 2009).

Foundation Degree Task Force (2004), *Report to Ministers*. London: DfES.

Fuller, A., Hodkinson, H., Hodkinson, P. and Unwin, L. (2005), 'Learning as peripheral participation in communities of practice: a reassessment of key concepts in workplace learning', *British Educational Research Journal*, 31 (1), 49–68.

Gagné, R. M. (1985), *The Conditions of Learning and Theory of Instruction*. (4th edn). Fort Worth, TX: Holt, Rinehart and Winston.

Gibbons, M., Limoges, C., Nowotny, H., Schwartzman, S., Scott, P. and Trow, M. (1994), *The New Production of Knowledge*. London: Sage.

Guile, D. and Young, M. (2001), 'Apprenticeship as a conceptual basis for a social theory of learning', in Paechter, C., Preedy, M., Scott, D. and Soler, J. (eds), *Knowledge, Power and Learning*. London: Paul Chapman /Open University Press, pp. 56–73.

Hanks, W. F. (1991), 'Foreword', in Lave, J. and Wenger, E., *Situated Learning: Legitimate Peripheral Participation*. Cambridge: Cambridge University Press, pp. 13–24.

Kolb, D. A. (1984), *Experiential Learning: Experience as the Source of Learning and Development*. New Jersey: Prentice-Hall.

Lave, J. and Wenger, E. (1991), *Situated Learning: Legitimate Peripheral Participation*. Cambridge: Cambridge University Press.

Lohman, M. C. (2000), 'Environmental inhibitors to informal learning in the workplace: a case study of public school teachers', *Adult Education Quarterly*, 50 (2), 83–101.

Lyotard, J. F., Bennington, G. and Massumi, B. (1984), *The Postmodern Condition: A Report on Knowledge. (Theory and History of Literature)*. Manchester: Manchester University Press.

McGill, I. and Beaty, L. (2001), *Action Learning: A Guide for Professional, Management and Educational Development*. London: Kogan Page.

McGill, I. and Brockbank, A. (2004), *The Action Learning Handbook: Powerful Techniques for Education, Professional Development and Training*. London: RoutledgeFalmer.

Moon, J. A. (1999), *Reflection in Learning and Professional Development: Theory and Practice*. London: RoutledgeFalmer.

Piaget, J. (1953), *The Origin of Intelligence in the Child*. London: Routledge and Kegan Paul.

QAA (2010), *Foundation Degree: Qualification Benchmark*. Gloucester: QAA.

Raelin, J. A. (2000), *Work-Based Learning: The New Frontier of Management Development*. New Jersey: Prentice Hall.

Rogers, A. (2002), 'Learning and adult education', in Harrison, R., Reeve, F., Hanson, A. and Clarke, J. (eds), *Supporting Lifelong Learning: Volume 1, Perspectives on Learning*. London: RoutledgeFalmer, pp. 8–24.

Schön D. A. (1983), *The Reflective Practitioner*. London: Temple Smith.

— (1987), *Educating the Reflective Practitioner*. London: Temple Smith.

Tennant, M. (2000), 'Learning to work, working to learn: theories of situational education', in Symes, C. and McIntyre, J. (eds), *Working Knowledge: The New Vocationalism and Higher Education*. Buckingham, UK: SRHE/Open University Press, pp. 123–134.

Wenger, E. (1998), *Communities of Practice: Learning, Meaning, and Identity*. Cambridge: Cambridge University Press.

— (2002), 'Communities of practice and social learning systems', in Reeve, F., Cartwright, M. and Edwards, R. (eds), *Supporting Lifelong Learning, Volume 2: Organizing Learning*. London: RoutledgeFalmer, pp. 160–179.

3 Issues for Learners

Hazel Kent and Jane Sharp

This chapter will:

- explore the learning needs of Foundation Degree students
- examine mechanisms for supporting learners as they prepare for study in higher education, during their programme and onwards to honours and other professional qualifications
- analyse the role of learning development and the rationale for ongoing, embedded study skills support
- consider the support of students with dyslexia and other specific learning differences.

Learner profiles

Statistics reveal that two discrete groups of students embark on Foundation Degrees: the first are full-time, male, under 25 years of age, with traditional Level 3 entry qualifications; in contrast, the second group are part-time, female, mature, and with a diverse range of entry qualifications (QAA, 2005). Sixty-four per cent of Foundation Degree students are female (HEFCE, 2010). These two disparate groups are unified by the 'defining characteristic' of Foundation Degree students: their identity as widening participation students (QAA, 2005). Indeed, the notion of the Foundation Degree as a widening participation tool was discussed in Chapter 1.

It has been argued that their broad profile is 'sufficiently different to the average FE or HE student that their differing needs be recognised and met' (Warner, 2004, p. 31). These needs particularly include issues regarding academic and information and communications technology (ICT) skills, self-esteem, confidence and time management of varied commitments (Shaw, 2004, p. 127; Warner, 2004, p. 31; Harvey, 2009, p. 56). A review of studies which examined Foundation Degree students' experiences (Harvey, 2009, p. 57) suggested that when they struggled:

> Much of the problem relates to pedagogic models, the nature of academic support (or lack of it) and the presumption about what constitutes autonomous learning in the university sector.

The need to explicitly teach study skills in the climate of a more diverse student population has been accepted within the UK Higher Education system since the early 1990s (Gosling, 2003; Burns and Sinfield, 2004). It is widely recognized that the majority of students do not enter higher education (HE) with the necessary study skills (Alston et al., 2008, p. 6). Equipping students with the 'necessary skills and attributes to succeed' is seen as 'a vital aspect of implementing foundation degrees' (Shaw, 2004, p. 125).

Meeting learning needs

Institutions have responded to this need to develop study skills in varied ways. Most have employed non-disciplinary support specialists, who are usually deployed in either centralized advice units or are aligned to particular faculties. Early approaches relied on remedial support for those 'non-traditional' students who were viewed as deficient in the skills required to succeed in HE (Cottrell, 2001). Those working in this emergent field of Learning Development now adopt a critical stance to this 'bolt-on' method of provision, and instead seek to form partnerships with academic staff to embed the teaching of these skills within the curriculum (Bailey, 2010). The aim of Learning Developers is to empower 'all students through the enhancement of their academic practices' (LearnHigher, 2009). Where fully implemented, this reflects an approach to widening participation which transforms the prevailing institutional culture in response to the increased diversity of the student body, rather than expecting students to be assimilated into a static, traditional system through socialization and osmosis (Shaw et al., 2007; Alston et al., 2008). Burns and Sinfield (2004, p. 20) articulate this as: 'the evolution of an emancipatory pedagogy that reveals the forms and process of academic discourse.' This chapter will explore the ways Learning Developers and academic staff can approach meeting Foundation Degree students' learning needs.

Pre-enrolment: preparing for study

To maximize the benefit which learners derive from their Foundation Degree experience, the diversity of their educational backgrounds and the specific needs of part-time and work-based learners can be addressed from pre-enrolment. Foregrounding awareness of likely issues and promoting student engagement with the support mechanisms available throughout their studies is thus a continuous project, rather than an induction-only activity, beginning with students' first contact with the institution, perhaps at open events, and continuing through to graduation and beyond.

The numbers of Foundation Degree students are anticipated to reach 100,000 in 2010–2011 (HEFCE, 2010, p. 2), and although they are often characterized as mature, female, with few traditional qualifications and studying part-time, they are a far from homogenous body as has already been noted. Corney et al. (2008, in Yorke and Longden 2010, p. 50) refer to part-time education for younger people as the 'forgotten child'. The specific employment- and/or sector-focused nature of Foundation Degrees may mean that students on any individual programme do not represent the range of educational and social backgrounds of the sector as a whole. There will be some overlap in terms of pre-enrolment concerns between the various groups of students, but also some significant differences. The specific demands of part-time and work-based study do require consideration, however, and this is a recurrent theme throughout this book.

An issue frequently associated with part-time study is that of juggling the demands of work, study and domestic roles. Indeed Yorke and Longden entitled their study of the experiences of part-time Foundation Degree students *Learning, Juggling and Achieving*. They found that the combination of demands placed upon Foundation Degree students was more challenging than the academic workload, although that was acknowledged as harder than expected (2010, p. 36). Similarly, Dunne et al. (2008, p. 55) note that 'greater recognition needs to be given to the sacrifices, challenges and conflicting commitments that face working, mature students'.

York and Longden (2010, p. 52) make a number of recommendations for institutions in recognition of the needs of part-time work-based students, including the provision of 'timely' information about course operation and making expectations of students explicit. They conclude that there will be a need for a fairly lengthy period of 'transition' into the process of higher education.

Case study: introduction to higher education taster courses

Taster courses are an established mechanism for easing mature and non-traditional learners into higher education. Bishop Grosseteste University College Lincoln has had a regular pattern of taster provision for a number of years which specifically targets prospective Foundation Degree learners.

Each taster session, usually an afternoon or evening, is divided into three sections, led by a different tutor and involves:

- Studying in higher education: focusing on expectations, jargon-busting, who's who, important documents, exploring anxieties and suggesting things to do over the summer to prepare for HE entry.
- Learning development: including an outline of the support available, an introduction to academic writing and a learner needs-assessment.
- ICT: involving an outline of the University College's IT services, discussion of the types of software applications and web facilities used and a discussion of personal skill levels.

⇨

The courses, arranged several months prior to entry, begin a process in which students are encouraged to disclose and discuss their concerns. Students describe the confidence boost derived from the knowledge that their concerns are shared by many of their colleagues:

'I learnt that I'm not the only one to have anxieties and that there is support available in several different areas.'

'The most useful aspect was knowing how many mature students there are and feeling reassured there will be plenty of support in my return to education.'

In some cases course tutors, learning advisors and e-learning specialists are able to directly address concerns and suggest actions; in others, reassurance is gained from articulating issues and realizing that they are shared by peers. In some instances peers themselves propose arrangements which will serve to facilitate time and space for learning.

These events often result in early disclosure of specific learning needs, accelerating the process of addressing them. Harvey and Drew, in their 2006 study of Early Years Sector Endorsed Foundation Degree students found that having special needs which were not met by the higher education institution were among factors cited by students for withdrawal from their programme.

The rationale for the provision of taster courses is that students' failure to access available support mechanisms in a timely manner could result in underachievement among learners and might ultimately result in students dropping out. Barber et al., writing about these sessions in 2006, suggest that merely informing students of the nature and availability of support is insufficient and that factors which inhibit take up include the tacit admission on the part of students that they may not be able to cope academically and that this would prejudice tutors' views of them. Thus, encouraging the articulation of such issues in a supportive environment may go some way towards ameliorating such concerns.

Factors affecting readiness to study

A number of factors affect readiness to study, including:

- awareness of the nature of higher education and the production of knowledge
- motivation, confidence or otherwise related to previous educational experiences
- recognition of relevant personal strengths and attributes.

The concept of knowledge in higher education as tacit, challengeable and changing is likely to be as unfamiliar to Foundation Degree students in the context of learning as it is to more traditional entrants. However, work-based students may be considered to be already embedded in their subject (e.g. refer to the discussion in Chapter 2 around work-based learning and forms of knowledge) and, to an extent, its discourse, and to be uniquely placed to utilize research and theoretical perspectives to examine and develop their practice thereby creating the climate for the promotion of deep learning (see e.g. Ramsden, 2003; Entwistle, 2009). Inducting students into this way of thinking and working as independent learners will need to be staged, supported and clearly articulated. Lack of confidence in academic ability is considered to be a significant barrier to achievement in higher education (Entwistle, 2009, pp. 28–32).

A valuable way of helping learners prepare for their Foundation Degree studies is to explore with them their motivation for study, to provide opportunities to value previous successes and confront negative experiences. Indeed, Harvey's (2009, p. 41) literature review of research on Foundation Degrees concludes that motivation to study is a key factor in Foundation Degree success. The most important motivator for undertaking study for mature students is career advancement, with career relevance and course content influencing uptake; whereas younger students are more likely than older colleagues to study Foundation Degrees for academic interest (2009, p. 43). Links with employers, location of institution and timing of classes also influence motivation to study. These findings are echoed by a recent study of part-time Foundation Degree students which found that the majority of students were studying because they needed a higher education qualification to progress in their career (Callender, 2010, p. 10). This aligns exactly with the aims of Foundation Degrees to provide learners with skills and knowledge relevant to their employment, as outlined in Chapter 1.

Many Foundation Degree students approach their studies from positions of low self-esteem and with backgrounds of negative formal educational experiences (e.g. Yorke and Longden, 2010). Nevertheless, all learners bring significant successes with them to their learning in higher education, although they might not always recognize their value or relevance. These might include learning to drive, to cook, to play a musical instrument, to grow vegetables or to play rugby. Each of these activities involve the bringing together of knowledge and skills in an applied situation and the likely involvement of reflection, practice and revision of techniques as learning proceeds. Similarly, some students may be involved in teaching children to read, or to ride a bicycle, or in coaching football or dance, bringing together not only the application of knowledge and understanding, but the clear articulation of these to the learner. Students with work-based experience may have worked in teams, to deadlines, met specific objectives, reported on progress and problems and worked towards solving these issues. Those with home and caring responsibilities will be expert organizers, planners, mediators, budgeters and time-managers.

To avoid what Wareing (2008) noted from a small pilot study of five healthcare Foundation Degree students was a 'terrifying, frightening' arrival at university, it may be appropriate to facilitate students' educational self-image through achievement-recognition and learning needs-assessment prior to arrival. Needs assessment is a valuable starting point, not least because students who lack confidence in academic and/ or IT skills, may be reassured that they bring a host of valuable knowledge, understanding and skills to their higher education experience. An example of study skills self-assessment can be found in Appendix 2.

Support available to students

There is a wealth of study skills resources available to students and it may be appropriate to direct those who wish to towards a selected few before they begin their studies formally. This needs to be undertaken with caution as the aim is to build confidence, not to overwhelm and deskill. Further, and as already discussed, Gibbs (2009) for example, reminds us that research consistently draws attention to the failure of discrete study skills interventions in higher education, reinforcing the need for these to be developed holistically as part of the developing discourse of the programme.

Reflection point: what study skills resources do you provide/recommend to your Foundation Degree students?

- The classic text for higher education study skills remains Cottrell's *Study Skills Handbook* (2008) and students can access some of these materials, plus audio and interactive resources at the link, Skills4Study website www.skills4study.com

---

- The Open University has a range of study skills units, such as Learning How to Learn, openlearn.open.ac.uk/index.php and select Skills. These require some investment of time, but can be usefully accessed before a programme commences.
- LearnHigher's excellent resources for students cover most aspects of academic practice. www.learnhigher.ac.uk/Students.html

Learning development, which is considered in detail later, is one of a range of support mechanisms available to higher education students to help them become independent learners. Much of this support is located within, provided under the auspices of, or facilitated by, the Foundation Degree provider, though employers can be a significant, if variable, source of support for work-based students.

Students are likely to form their first and strongest bond within an institution through their **course tutors**. Jackson and Tunnan (2005, in Harvey, 2009) acknowledge the value Foundation Degree students place on this relationship and its role in retention. Some students struggle with the multi-faceted nature of the higher education tutors' role: as experts in their field, as facilitators of learning rather than as founts of knowledge and as assessors of learning, although this is no more an adjustment for a Foundation Degree student than for any other. Key to the success of the course tutor-Foundation Degree student relationship will be familiarity with and empathy with the specific needs of these learners.

For very many students, whatever their background and confidence level, engaging with the **library** can be a daunting process. Most Foundation Degree students will have limited time in the institution, much of it heavily timetabled, and this can prove a further disincentive to engage with the many powerful and complex research facilities available to them. Students will need opportunities to build confident relationships with library staff, whether face-to-face or electronically, through staged engagement with facilities. The challenges of managing and making sense of the vast array of resources available are further highlighted by the time constraints of work-based students. Students can be encouraged to seek assistance and library services alerted to the often limited times such students will have available to seek support. Warner (2004, p. 31) notes that access to library and electronic databases may be further complicated for Foundation Degree students studying in partner further education colleges as, although students may have access rights to the awarding higher education institution's databases and portals, locally based library staff may not.

Virtual learning environments (VLEs) are an important part of student life in the twenty-first century; more so for part-time and work-based students, as failure to access them completely may isolate students from areas of their studies and, just as importantly, from interaction with their peers. Many students have very real concerns related to their own IT literacy, specifications for computers, requirements for internet access and so forth. Access to e-learning specialists and advice can empower students and build confidence (e-learning is discussed more fully in Chapter 6).

Financial issues have been repeatedly identified as significant obstacles for Foundation Degree students (e.g. Greenwood et al., 2008). The institution's **student support** service can enable students to obtain their funding entitlements and budget accordingly. Similarly maintaining contact with students whose circumstances may change can be an issue in retention. Student support usually also provide a wealth of other welfare services to students and again prioritizing accessible appointments, particularly at times such as the start of the academic year can be vital.

Students also identify **employer support** as being a significant factor in success (QAA, 2005), particularly the role of the workplace mentor. Yorke and Longden typify this employer support as 'proactive' and characterized by engaging actively with studies, answering questions and providing feedback, or 'responsive' by, for example, providing time off to study (2010, p. 38). Therefore, partnership working between the FE and/or HE institution and the employer is crucial for a rounded work-based learning experience. In this respect, formal agreements between institution and employer can play an important role in clarifying the roles and responsibilities of all parties. Chapter 4 contains a discussion around work-based learning agreements.

The contribution of **peer and group interaction** is significant for this group of learners. It is of particular importance for part-time and distance students, and there is a clear role for tutors and programme designers in facilitating this interaction. Yorke and Longden (2010, p. 22) found that Foundation Degree students rated the network and/or social aspect of study. Students, in their sample, who had completed half or more of their studies engaged more with fellow students, possibly as a result of experience and the development of friendship and working groups and practices. They characterize this as the 'community' aspect of learning and note the value that students attach to it, cautioning how-ever that, 'the dominant culture in higher education reflects a view of learning that focuses on the individual, with the social aspect being backgrounded' (2010, p. 43).

An institution's **careers service** will have a role to play. Most students undertake Foundation Degree studies to improve their chances of career progression, as noted earlier. Some, of course, may need to find new positions, paid or voluntary, during their course. However, Callender et al. (2010, p. 55) found that only 30 per cent of part-time Foundation Degree students accessed their institution's careers service. This was in part because students had clear career plans associated with their stud-ies and did not require advice, although a significant minority did not realize that the institution had a careers service or that this was available to part-time students already in employment.

Reflection point

Consider the sources of support outlined above: study skills resources; learning development; course tutors; the library; virtual learning environments; student sup-port services; employers; the students' peer group; careers advice. What is your role in ensuring that they are used effectively to support student learning?

The role of Learning Developers

Learning Developers provide support to Foundation Degree students in several forms, which will vary according to institutional culture and organizational structures. Broadly, most will offer one-to-one tutori-als, resources for self-help, drop-in sessions, and workshops. For some this will also extend into involvement with academic staff development. This portfolio of provision recognizes that 'the increasing diversity of the student body calls for multiple strategies' and allows for individual choice (Hill et al., 2010). The range of skills developed is extensive and can include the following:

- academic writing, including referencing and avoiding plagiarism, planning, structuring, vocabulary, argument and critical analysis
- skills for effective proof-réading, including spelling, punctuation and grammar, sentence construction and paragraphs
- broader study skills, such as time management, effective reading and literature searching, note-making and revision strategies.

For Foundation Degree students, accessing these services may not be as straightforward as for full-time undergraduates. Being on campus for perhaps only one heavily timetabled day per week obviously limits the time available to access the full range of university resources, as noted by Warner (2004, p. 31). Consequently, Learning Developers recognize the need to offer their services flexibly, for example by prioritizing appointment slots, offering email and telephone consultations or providing online self-help materials. It is also important to recognize that demand for advice on learning does not only occur at the beginning of courses. Knight et al. (2006, p. 6) found that support of this nature provided by lecturers declined by the end of the first year, as they began to expect more autonomous learning. Although some students in their study felt this expectation of independence to be entirely appropriate, 'others had felt abandoned' (Knight et al. 2006, p. 6). In this scenario, Learning Development services can be successfully utilized to differentiate with a continuum of support for those students who require it. However, it is important to emphasize that just as subject knowledge develops throughout courses, so do academic skills and practices, and consequently course design should reflect this. Shaw (2004, p. 138) concluded that for Foundation Degree students, 'this area needs width, depth and length to be successfully implemented.'

Learning Development tutorials offer students a space to discuss their work with a specialist skills adviser, who will not be involved in assessing their work. Experience has shown that Foundation Degree students who have chosen to utilize tutorial provision value the opportunities provided, and it is argued that such tutorials facilitate learning by providing a non-threatening reflexive environment which is conducive to building self-esteem.

> **Learner voice**
>
> I found my trip to Learning Advice beneficial for all assignments which followed the one I initially sought advice about. It was friendly, non-judgemental and confidence-boosting. As a mature student with a family and work commitments, who is on campus for one day a week only, it's great to know that you're there for support when it's needed! (Foundation Degree Student)

However, research completed at Brunel University (Donnarumma and Gill, 2007) suggested that those mature students who had decided not to engage with Learning Development regarded such services negatively, as they 'diminished proper pride in their own coping skills and capacities'. Sutcliffe et al. (2005, p. 46) reinforce this, commenting that:

> Support can be in place, however, if the learners do not see this as useful, or if they've had difficulty in accessing the support, then the perceptions of support will be widely different between the learners and the providers.

As early as 2001, Cottrell argued that this tendency could be overcome by the creation of an institutional culture which encourages all students to consider their learning development needs. Partly this involves the positive promotion of Learning Development services by tutors and lecturers, but on a deeper level it requires a committed institutional embrace of an embedded approach to teaching academic skills and practices, to which discussion we will now turn.

Embedding academic skills within Foundation Degree courses

Debate within the Learning Development community has recently focused on how their work should evolve, and specifically how it should be embedded within courses (Hilsdon, 2010). It is now accepted across the sector that study skills taught in isolation are not as effective as those contextualized within the students' subject areas. It has been argued that this is particularly important for Foundation Degree students, as time is limited on the course, and students are necessarily very focused on practical learning relating to employability issues rather than learning for its own sake (Shaw, 2004, p. 128). Aside from issues relating to student motivation, there is a significant learning justification for embedding. An academic literacies approach to embedding teaching on academic writing is currently idealized as preferable to both the separate teaching of study skills and the expectation that skills will develop through academic socialization (Lea and Street, 1998; Wingate, 2006; Alston et al., 2008). This rests upon a theoretical understanding of writing as part of the epistemological process within subject areas, rather than as a technical skill which can be acquired separately, and explains why students have such difficulty in transferring skills acquired elsewhere (Lea and Street, 1998). On a more pragmatic note, Blake and Pates (2010) have noted that universities are increasingly aware of the high cost of individualized support for a large number of students, adding an economic motivation to the impetus to embed. However, although this model for embedding the development of academic skills has been identified and advocated repeatedly, in practice the complex organizational, institutional and pedagogical issues it raises can be significant barriers to its implementation (Ganobcsik-Williams, 2006).

The embedding of study skills into Foundation Degrees is an under-researched area. In one of the few studies to do so, Shaw (2004, p. 126) highlighted that 'introducing study skills was a matter of considerable subtlety and complexity'. Consequently, communication and partnership between subject specialist academics and learning developers is vital, at the level of curriculum planning as well as regarding delivery. Working with educational development colleagues has also been advocated (Gibbs, 2009). In practice it is recognized that initiatives to embed are often very small scale and dependent on complex institutional and professional relationships (Hill et al., 2010). It is argued that where successful, they can then be used as models and expanded (Gibson and Myers, 2010; Hill et al., 2010). With regard to students, Shaw (2004) observed that key to encouraging them to take the skills taught seriously is the need to assess them explicitly. This emphasis on explicit assessment is substantiated by the influential work undertaken at the University of Wollongong (Alston et al., 2008). This Australian university has worked since 1997 to develop a model of partnership between subject academics and Learning Developers (Alston et al., 2008). Significantly, this involves a collaborative approach to assessment and evaluation, as well as to planning and delivery.

However, in the light of the difficulties involved in embedding, it remains crucial to provide a multi-strategy approach to the teaching of academic writing and study skills, to ensure the diverse needs of all students are met (Hill et al., 2010). Particularly, it is suggested that provision involving one-to-one Learning Development tutorials should be retained, as in practice this often involves close formative work based on the text of students' current assignments, which, in a mass HE system, subject tutors rarely have the opportunity to engage in. Lillis (in Ganobcsik-Williams 2006, p. 43) has argued that dialogue based on students' writing should be based at the centre of an academic literacies pedagogy. In this sense, Learning Development style tutorials which are based on current assignments are naturally embedded, as exemplified in the following session plan.

Embedded co-taught session plan

Course: FdA Children's Services (Early Childhood)	Tutors: Module Leader Learning Adviser
Time/Date: 1 hour, May 2010	Level: 4
Aims	To prepare students for undertaking a time limited assignment (TLA)
Learning outcomes	Students have knowledge of effective study skills to employ when preparing and taking a TLA. Students have identified and begun to revise specific content for this TLA
Resources	
Activities	PowerPoint presentation; interactive whiteboard; handout
Learning Adviser	Lead presentation on how to prepare a TLA. Respond to student questions about effective study practices
Module leader	Contribute to presentation by providing contextualized examples from course content on preparing for this specific TLA. Respond to student questions about module content and revision
Students	Note taking; asking questions; contribute to discussion during brainstorm activities on revision strategies

Evaluation:

This co-taught session worked very effectively. Students who attended were appreciative of the advice given and attained higher than anticipated marks in the TLA. The combination of expertise provided by the Module Leader and the Learning Adviser ensured the session provided an appropriate balance of skills-based advice with subject specific contextualization. This ensured that the session was relevant and appropriate to the students' immediate development needs. Students were encouraged to ask questions and seek clarification during the session, and were also reminded of how to seek individual/small group follow-up sessions if anxieties were not satisfied. The session will be timetabled again in 2011.

Supporting students with specific learning difficulties

Students with Specific Learning Differences (SpLDs) such as dyslexia particularly require regular and specialized support to achieve their potential as learners in higher education (HE). The 2001 Special Needs and Disability Act (SENDA) amended the 1995 Disability Discrimination Act (DDA) to encompass education. Notably, SENDA includes an anticipatory clause, which requires institutions to consider and reflect on their provision in the event of any student applying, rather than just focusing on the needs of current students (Hall, 2007, p. 131). Despite this, research has shown that the student experience of those with SpLDs is not always positive (Griffin and Pollak, 2009). With specific regard to Foundation Degrees, it has been observed that students with dyslexia have often had negative previous experiences of education, and consequently need substantially more support than their neurotypical peers to raise levels of self-esteem and confidence (Lewis-Hobbs, 2010).

Students with SpLDs belong to one of two groups: those who are aware of their learning difference when applying and those who only become aware of their learning difference while at university. For the first group, the students concerned have often had substantial previous experience in dealing with their SpLD and are at the advantage of being able to arrange the support required before they start their course. Students attend assessment centres to have their needs assessed. Universities typically have centralized disability support services which assist applications for the Disabled Students Allowance (DSA), facilitate reasonable adjustments, and communicate with lecturers. Specialist assistance can include, for example, tutorials, the provision of computer equipment and software, and additional time in exams. For the second group, diagnosis occurs while at university. Lecturers sometimes suggest there may be an issue, sometimes the issue is raised during learning development tutorials, or talking to friends might be a trigger. Some, particularly mature students, seem to have had long-held suspicions, but only decide to act once it becomes a barrier to their course. As this is a significant issue, the British Dyslexia Association (BDA) advocates incorporating a simple self-assessment checklist into induction programmes (BDA,

2010). In the first instance many universities may be able to provide a screening, which will indicate whether an Educational Psychologist's assessment is required. Where a diagnosis is confirmed, students will then enter the process of applying for the DSA, needs assessment, and making arrangements for the adjustments required. In addition, such students often face considerable emotional issues in coming to terms with their newly acquired label. For some it is a relief, and provides a welcome explanation of a history of educational difficulties. For others, their reaction is far more complex and this requires careful support.

Learner voice

The course was not too bad until I got my first grade back – I failed. I felt really down about it and thought I might have to drop out. On the bottom of the feed-back sheet it said to go to Learning Advice and I was pleased there was a chance of help. But when it was suggested that I might be dyslexic I was upset. I hadn't thought there was a problem before – my general reading and writing were fine, but the style of reading and writing on the course was completely different – I've had to learn a whole new style. I knew I didn't remember things I'd read and would sometimes have to read things three or more times, and this was just really hard on the course because of the amount of reading.

I went to [the dyslexia support tutor] for a screening and it helped to know there was support there. Going to see the Educational Psychologist was scary – I was with him for about four hours but felt rushed on a lot of the tests and think I would have got more right if I'd had more time to look at some of the reading tasks. It was hard to get over being told I'd suddenly got dyslexia, I think it was fear of the unknown. Talking to [the dyslexia support tutor] helped me come to terms with it, and I also got friendly with another dyslexic student, that has been really helpful. Does it change you? It doesn't in a way; you're always the same because you've always had it – just didn't know about it before. I did recognize the qualities of dyslexia in myself when they were explained to me. But I was worried about how other people would judge me and how they have a lack of understanding what it means.

I started getting support for my writing straightaway and learnt most from the comments and suggestions given on my written work – mostly learning the right academic words – I tend to write in simple words – my brain doesn't know the academic words. I feel really positive when I send my work in and my marks have gone up. The comments are getting fewer and I know I'm improving. I like being able to contact my support tutor quickly and get a response quickly when I'm really struggling. It helps to be able to come in and talk to her face to face. The other support method I use a lot is being able to scan the reading into the computer and hear it read to me. That way I can pick out the bits that I need – without it I wouldn't be able to cope. Even with that I don't always do the recommended reading every week – I find the amount of reading too much. Without the support I would have definitely dropped out. I have to work harder than the others – it takes longer to complete assignment and I have to get them written earlier to be able to get the help with them. The exams are the worst part as I don't have the support with my writing in them and I failed one last semester because of my difficulties with writing.

I still don't find it easy to tell people about being dyslexic – I am afraid they will judge me. I didn't want to tell work but they found out, and my manager is not very understanding – she thinks it means I will not cope with promotion and I think I might have to go elsewhere to go further. I want to do the top up year but am worried I won't be able to as there are so many people who are better than me. I can't wait for my Foundation Degree graduation though – and the buzz that will go through when my family see me up there! It's in my diary in bright red.

Dyslexic Foundation Degree students are unlikely to have had previous experience of higher level writing and study skills, and therefore require considerable support to utilize strategies which enable them to study effectively at this level (Lewis-Hobbs, 2010). In addition to individualized support from specialized tutors, these students can also be supported by the adoption of certain practices by their course tutors. The following strategies are among the excellent advice on teaching dyslexic students in HE provided by the British Dyslexia Association (BDA, 2010):

- create a clearly prioritized two-stage reading list to mitigate difficulties with reading, particularly skimming and scanning skills
- consider how information is presented – use Sans serif fonts for text, such as Arial, with a minimum size of 12pt
- for some dyslexic learners, it is important to consider the colour of paper used, or background colour for slides on PowerPoint presentations
- explicitly introduce new vocabulary when teaching and use visuals, such as pictures, diagrams and charts, to assist these learners
- most importantly, tutors should communicate with individuals and discover how they learn most effectively.

Although dyslexia is the most common learning difference among students in HE, the number of students with a range of other learning differences is increasing (Griffin and Pollak, 2009). Students with dyspraxia, dyscalculia, dysgraphia, Asperger's, AD(H)D, Tourette syndrome, Meares-Irlen and mental health issues are becoming more prevalent in HE (BRAINHE, 2010). Hearing and visual impairments also impact students' learning and have implications for teaching and assessment.

Reflection point

How extensive is your knowledge of specific learning difficulties? Are you aware of students with particular difficulties? Are your approaches to learning, teaching and assessment fully accessible for these learners? Could accessibility be improved in any way?

In most HEIs, disability support specialists provide invaluable advice for both students and tutors. In addition, useful sector specific guidance for tutors and students can be found at the following websites:

SCIPS (Strategies for Creating Inclusive Programmes of Study) www.scips.worc. ac.uk

BRAINHE (Best resources for achievement and intervention re Neurodiversity in Higher Education) www.brainhe.com

Tutors should also consider the accessibility of assessment for students with specific learning disabilities and this is discussed in Chapter 7.

Progression beyond the Foundation Degree

Among the distinctive characteristics of Foundation Degrees described in the QAA benchmark (2010) is the provision of progression and 'articulation' routes for graduates in the form of honours degrees, professional qualifications and higher NVQs. HEFCE (2010, p. 43) reports that of the cohort gaining Foundation Degrees from HEIs in 2007–2008, 59 per cent of full-time and 43 per cent of part-time students progressed immediately to an honours degree programme, mostly at the same institution. Of these students 67 per cent graduated within a year; 35 per cent with a first or upper second degree (2010, p. 46). Articulation to honours degree level can be achieved either through a purpose-designed progression course, equivalent to one year's full-time study, or by joining an existing undergraduate honours programme at Level 6, usually the third year.

QAA (2008, p. 19) characterize the specific demands of study at honours level (HE Level 6) as requiring:

- an understanding of a complex body of knowledge, some of it at the current boundaries of an academic discipline
- analytical techniques and problem-solving skills that can be applied in many types of employment
- the ability to evaluate evidence, arguments and assumptions, to reach sound judgements and to communicate them effectively.

The HE Level 6 work is usually accompanied by an expectation that students will already be encultured into both the 'academy' and the discourse of the discipline, with corresponding expectations in terms of critical reading, research techniques, academic writing and self-directed learning. QAA Reviews' (2005, p. 34) recommendations include 'provision of a match between the modes of study on the articulated honours degree with the modes of study on the Foundation Degree'.

Penketh and Goddard (2008, p. 316) note that the transition experience for Foundation Degree graduates in Learning Support reflected not merely a change in academic expectations but a shift from an essentially work-based programme to one with 'greater theoretical and critical engagement'. They acknowledge that even where the articulation route is part-time it may represent a change of learning location, from online to face-to-face and/or from partnership FEC to HEI. The shift in academic requirements from Level 5 to Level 6 are no greater for Foundation Degree graduates than for transitional undergraduates, but they are often coupled with new locations, peers, tutors and support mechanisms. Furthermore there is likely no role for the workplace mentor, an additional adjustment for students.

Greenbank (2007, in Harvey, 2009, p. 54) conducted research centred on the experiences of Foundation Degree graduates from FECs articulating to an honours programme at one new university. He found that teaching and learning styles (more lectures, fewer small group discussions) were among stress factors noted by students. Accessibility and attitudes of lecturers were also significant issues. Harvey (2009) takes issue with at least part of Greenbank's analysis, suggesting that his conclusion that Foundation Degree graduates are not equipped for autonomous learning is based on an acceptance of traditional approaches to teaching and learning in universities, the implication being that the university should be more student-centred in meeting and matching the needs of its students, echoing Dixon et al. (2005).

Summary

Foundation Degree students have particular learning strengths and needs when they enter higher education. Maximizing student outcomes requires an integrated, coherent and flexible approach to support from both academic and support departments. To be effective, academic skills development should be carefully embedded throughout Foundation Degree programmes: a process which begins at the planning stage of the degree, and which is the focus of Chapter 4.

References

Alston, F., Gourlay, L., Sutherland, R. and Thomson, K. (2008), *Introducing Scholarship Skills: Academic Writing*. Glasgow: QAA.

Bailey, R. (2010), 'The role and efficacy of generic learning and study support: what is the experience and perspective of academic teaching staff?' *Journal of Learning Development in Higher Education*, 2. Available online at: www.aldinhe.ac.uk/ojs/index.php?journal=jldhe&page=article&op=view&path%5B%5D=57&path%5B%5D=36 (accessed 30 August 2011).

Barber D., Richardson, L. and Taylor, C. (2006), 'An introduction to higher education: supporting the needs of Foundation Degree students', *Forward*, 10, 32–34. Available online at: www.fdf.ac.uk/downloads/142/20090813110150journal10.pdf (accessed 21 October 2010).

Blake, R. and Pates, J. (2010), 'Embedding report writing workshops into an undergraduate Environmental Science module through a subject specialist and learning developer partnership', *Journal of Learning Development in Higher Education*, 2. Available online at: www.aldinhe.ac.uk/ojs/index.php?journal=jldhe&page=article&op=view&path%5B%5D=43&path%5B%5D=30 (accessed 30 August 2011).

BRAINHE (2010), 'BRAINHE leaflet', Available online at: www.brainhe.com/students/types/leaflet.html (accessed 24 February 2011).

BDA (2010), 'Practical solutions for Further and Higher Education'. (Workshop 6 October 2010).

Burns, T. and Sinfield, S. (2004), *Teaching, Learning and Study Skills: A Guide for Tutors*. London: Sage.

Callender, C. (2010), 'Part-time Foundation Degree students: their reasons for studying, use of careers information, advice and guidance and how they pay for learning', *Forward*, 21, 9–13. Available online at: www.fdf.ac.uk/downloads/284/20100708161239journal%2021.pdf (accessed 21 October 2010).

Callender, C., Wilkinson, D. and Hopkin, R. (2010), *Career Decision Making and Career Development of Part-Time Foundation Degree Students*. Lichfield: Foundation Degree Forward. Available online at: www.fdf.ac.uk/downloads/277/20100611125050CareerDev%20PT%20FdStudents_fullreport.pdf (accessed 21 October 2010).

Cottrell, S. (2001), *Teaching Study Skills and Supporting Learning*. Basingstoke: Palgrave Macmillan.

— (2008), *The Study Skills Handbook*. Basingstoke: Palgrave Macmillan.

DDA (1995), *Disability Discrimination Act*. Available online at: www.legislation.gov.uk/ukpga/1995/50/contents (accessed 13 April 2011).

Dixon, J., Tripathi, S., Sanderson, A., Gray, C., Rosewall, I. and Sherriff, I. (2005), 'Accessible higher education: meeting the challenges of HE in FE', *Forward*, 6, 34–38. Available online at: www.fdf.ac.uk/downloads/138/20090813105554journal6.pdf (accessed 21 October 2010).

Donnarumma, D. and Gill, M. (2007), 'Perceptions of Learning Support or Advice', CETLs Research Symposium, Liverpool Hope University. 26 June 2007. Available online at: http://oro.open.ac.uk/17528/1/Perceptions_of_learning_support_or_advice.pdf (accessed 25 February 2011).

Dunne, L., Goddard, G. and Woodhouse, C. (2008), 'Mapping the changes: a critical exploration into the career trajectories of teaching assistants who undertake a foundation degree', *Journal of Vocational Education and Training*, 60 (1), 49–59.

Entwistle, N. (2009), *Teaching for Understanding at University*. Basingstoke: Palgrave Macmillan.

Ganobcsik-Williams, L. (2006), *Teaching Academic Writing in UK Higher Education*. Basingstoke: Palgrave.

Gibbs, G. (2009), 'Developing students as learners – varied phenomena, varied contexts and a developmental trajectory for the whole endeavour', *Journal of Learning Development in Higher Education*, 1. Available online at: www.aldinhe.ac.uk/ojs/index.php?journal=jldhe&page=article&op=view&path%5B%5D=30&path%5B%5D=14 (accessed 30 August 2011).

Gibson, F. and Myers, J. (2010), 'The fragmented route to a whole institution approach to integrating learning development. Reporting on a work in process', *Journal of Learning Development in Higher Education*, 2. Available online at: www.aldinhe.ac.uk/ojs/index.php?journal=jldhe&page=article&op=view&path%5B%5D=47&path%5B%5D=32 (accessed 30 August 2011).

Gosling, D. (2003), 'Supporting student learning', in Fry, H., Ketteridge, S. and Marshall, S. (eds), *A Handbook for Teaching and Learning in Higher Education*. London: RoutledgeFalmer.

Greenwood, M. and Little, B. with Burch, E., Collins, C., Kimura, M. and Yarrow, K. (2008), *Report to Foundation Degree Forward on the Impact of Foundation Degrees on Students and the Workplace*. London: Centre for Higher Education Research and Information, The Open University and the Learning and Skills Network.

Griffin, E. and Pollak, D. (2009), 'Student experiences of neurodiversity in higher education: insights from the BRAINHE project', *Dyslexia*, 15, 23–41.

Hall, W. (2007), 'Supporting students with disabilities in higher education', in Campbell, A. and Norton, L. (eds), *Learning, Teaching and Assessing in Higher Education: Developing Reflective Practice*. Exeter: Learning Matters.

Harvey, L. (2009), 'Review of research literature focused on Foundation Degree', *Foundation Degrees Forward*. Available online at: www.fdf.ac.uk/downloads/195/20090907102408Lee HarveyLitReview.pdf (accessed 28 September 2010).

Harvey, L. and Drew, S. with Smith, M. (2006), *The First-Year Experience: Review of the Research Literature*. York: Higher Education Academy. Available online at: www.heacademy.ac.uk/assets/York/documents/ourwork/archive/first_year_experience_full_report.pdf (accessed 21 October 2010).

HEFCE (2010), *Foundation Degrees: Key Statistics 2001–02 to 2009–10*. Available online at: www.hefce.ac.uk/pubs/hefce/2010/10_12 (accessed 21 October 2010).

Hill, P., Tinker, A. and Catterall, S. (2010), 'From deficiency to development: the evolution of academic skills provision at one UK university', *Journal of Learning Development in Higher Education*, 2, 1–19. Available online at: www.aldinhe.ac.uk/ojs/index.php?journal=jldhe&page=article&op=view&path%5B%5D=54&path%5B%5D=38 (accessed 30 August 2010).

Hilsdon, J. (2010), 'Reasons to be cheerful?' *Journal of Learning Development in Higher Education*, 2, 1–5. Available online at: www.aldinhe.ac.uk/ojs/index.php?journal=jldhe&page=index (accessed 14 April 2010).

Knight, T., Tennant, R., Dillon, L. and Weddell, E. (2006), *Evaluating the Early Years Sector Endorsed Foundation Degree: A Qualitative Study of Students' Views and Experiences*. Nottingham: DfES. Available online at: http://education.gov.uk/publications/eOrderingDownload/RR751.pdf (accessed 24 February 2011).

Lea, M. and Street, B. (1998), 'Student writing in higher education: an academic literacies approach', *Studies in Higher Education*, 23 (2), 157–173.

LearnHigher (2009), 'Learning Development'. Available online at: www.learnhigher.ac.uk/learningdevelopment.htm (accessed 16 February 2009).

Lewis-Hobbs, S. (2010), 'Supporting dyslexic foundation degree students'. (Interview) Bishop Grosseteste University College Lincoln.

Penketh, C. and Goddard, G. (2008), 'Students in transition: mature women students moving from Foundation Degree to Honours Level 6', *Research in Post-Compulsory Education*, 13 (3), 315–327.

QAA (2005), *Learning From Reviews of Foundation Degrees Carried Out in England in 2004–05: Sharing Good Practice*. Gloucester: QAA.

— (2008), *The Framework for Higher Education Qualifications in England, Wales and Northern Ireland*. Gloucester: QAA. Available online at: www.qaa.ac.uk/Publications/InformationAndGuidance/Documents/FHEQ08.pdf (accessed 30 August 2010).

— (2010), *Foundation Degree Qualification Benchmark*. Gloucester: QAA.

— Ramsden, P. (2003), *Learning to Teach in Higher Education*. (2nd edn). Abingdon: RoutledgeFalmer.

SENDA (2001), *Special Educational Needs and Disability Act*. Available online at: www.legislation.gov.uk/ukpga/2001/10/contents (accessed 13 April 2011).

Shaw, J. (2004), 'Embedding Study Skills Foundation Degree in travel and tourism', in Brennan, L. and Gosling, D. (eds), *Making Foundation Degrees Work*. Essex: SEEC.

Shaw, J., Brain, K., Bridger, K., Foreman, J. and Reid, I. (2007), *Embedding Widening Participation and Promoting Student Diversity*. Available online at: www.heacademy.ac.uk/assets/York/documents/resources/publications/embedding_wp_business_case_approach_july07.pdf (accessed 17 May 2009).

Sutcliffe, J. (2005), 'Developing a flexible delivery method for the foundation degree in teaching and learning support: a case study of Edge Hill', *Forward*, 6, 44–48. Available online at: www.fdf.ac.uk/downloads/138/20090813105554journal6.pdf (accessed 25 February 2011).

Wareing, M. (2008), 'Foundation Degree students as work-based learners: the mentor's role', *British Journal of Nursing*, 17 (8), 532–537.

Warner, J. (2004), 'Providing learning resource support to Foundation Degree students: a case study at Kingston College Learning Resources Centre', *Forward*, 3, 31–34. Available online at: www.fdf.ac.uk/downloads/135/20090813105240journal3.pdf (accessed 21 October 2010).

Wingate, U. (2006), 'Doing away with "study skills"', *Teaching in Higher Education*, 11 (4), 457–469.

Yorke, M. and Longden, B. (2010), *Learning Juggling and Achieving: Students Experiences of Part-time Foundation Degrees*. Lichfield: fdf. Available online at: www.fdf.ac.uk/downloads/228/20100125164438Yorke&LongdenReport.pdf (accessed 22 October 2010).

Course Design

Angela House and Claire Taylor

4

This chapter will:

- provide a holistic view on course design
- include advice on the validation process
- discuss the management of quality issues
- address student learning opportunities and engagement
- provide realistic guidance on engaging with employers.

Starting points

Proposals for new Foundation Degree programmes originate in a variety of places. You may be engaged with or by employers to advance and enhance their training provision, or perhaps an individual staff member or a senior manager in your institution has suggested an exciting and original idea. It may be that you have experience of a particular sector, and perceive an opportunity to advance the level of qualification in that sector. All these starting points represent valid ways into the course design process, but the key thing is that, however initiated, proposals for new programmes and the process of course design should not be developed and carried out in isolation. For example, proposals must support the institution's mission and corporate strategy, and you must have an understanding of the audience whose needs you will be addressing – designing a Foundation Degree is not a task to be rushed into unsuspectingly.

Reflection point

Who is the audience for your proposed course? Have you considered the needs and perspectives of the following stakeholders: students, employers, the validating institution, the course team, partners such as professional bodies, possibly public sector bodies or charitable/voluntary organizations?

The validation process

Your own HEI (or validating partner HEI if you are working within FE) will have guidelines, within a Code of Practice for the Validation of Programmes, which will take you through the validation process. This is the process for securing institutional approval for new programmes and it should conform to the provisions of the QAA's *Code of Practice for the Assurance of Academic Quality and Standards in Higher Education*, section 7: 'Programme Design, Approval, Monitoring and Review' (QAA, 2006). Check your institution's guidance carefully, but it is likely that the first stage will involve the completion of a programme proposal form or equivalent, which will ask you to consider all or some of the following:

- the institution's mission and corporate strategy
- the aims and outcomes of the programme
- the intended market and intended career opportunities for graduates
- the programme relationship to the FHEQ
- external reference points including the academic infrastructure

- requirements of any professional bodies involved
- consultation with employers, students or other stakeholders
- the need for assessment to clearly reflect the stated rationale and learning outcomes
- issues of level, progression, balance and overall coherence
- the available resources, financial and staffing implications.

Once the proposal has been approved (usually following scrutiny by an institutional committee) it can be progressed to validation. This will involve a series of events within the institution where course documentation is further scrutinized by both internal and external peers, students, employers and other stakeholders as appropriate. It is likely that at this stage you will be asked to present a Draft Programme Document, which is likely to contain sections such as:

- a programme specification (there will be a standard institutional pro forma for this)
- a rationale for the programme
- an account of the learning and teaching strategy to be adopted
- an overview of the resources available to support students' learning
- an account of the assessment strategy
- an overview of the arrangements for the management and organization of the programme
- the target student intake and an account of the steps that will be taken to maintain recruitment at that level
- an account of the admission requirements, the process for the selection of applicants and details of the way in which admissions procedures will take account of the institution's Diversity and Equality and Race Equality policies
- module specifications for each module (example pro forma in Appendix 3).

Coherency and quality assurance

In addition to the required content of the documentation outlined in the previous section (and specified within institutional guidance), the development team should keep in mind issues of balance in the programme content as a whole and the progression of students through the programme. Fundamental to ensuring that the programme is coherent is the need for clear alignment between the programme specification and module specifications and for the rationale, learning outcomes and assessment strategy to be correlated clearly. Biggs (1999) coined the term 'constructive alignment', the basic premise of which is that the curriculum is designed so that the learning activities and assessment tasks are aligned with the learning outcomes that are intended in the course. Biggs' approach is wholly student centred (Walsh, 2007) and is built around the idea that students construct meaning from their learning experiences as opposed to tutors simply imparting meaning. This model would appear to fit seamlessly into the work-based learning model of Foundation Degrees, in which students meet potential learning experiences on a daily basis in their workplace settings.

One way to approach this is to consider the idea of 'learning styles'. Recognizing that the ways in which individuals learn will differ, the alignment of learning outcomes and assessment should provide different opportunities for all to gain and demonstrate understanding; it should also be understood that it would be unrealistic to meet the needs of all individuals at the same time. Therefore academic staff should ensure that there are a variety of opportunities incorporated into their learning and teaching strategy, using a mixture of teaching approaches in planning the sessions to be advantageous to the highest number of students.

In order that the assurance of quality is built into course design from the outset, early consultation is advised with the Academic Quality office within the HEI – this is where you will find guidance on regulations and codes of practice which govern any degree, undertaken, validated and awarded at the HEI. Regulations regarding the validation have already been mentioned, but you will also need to consult codes of practice related to:

- work-based and placement learning
- collaborative provision (if you are part of an HE-FE partnership)
- flexible and distributed learning (e.g. if the course involves distance learning)
- assessment
- disabled students.

QAA Codes of Practice related to these areas are available on the QAA website, as is the Foundation Degree benchmark statement (QAA, 2010) and other subject benchmark statements which may be of relevance to the course you are designing.

Reflection point

- Do you monitor government policy in workforce development, especially in areas of your expertise? You will need to convince the institution that there is an audience/need for the Foundation Degree.
- Have you discretely researched what is being offered by other institutions in your local area? This can establish areas of need for development.
- Have you checked out local industry/authority interest in training and development?
- You need to make contact with the local industry/authority/institutions to establish links. These may form stakeholder groups later – see the next section on 'Employer Engagement'.
- Have you checked staff interests and areas of expertise? Are there any gaps in subject knowledge/expertise? This may make the programme vulnerable and difficult for institutions to resource.
- Are you clear about quality procedures at your institution and/or a collaborative HEI? This can save time in developing the programme proposals, and taking the programme to validation.
- Are you familiar with relevant codes of practice, regulations, strategies and any sector-specific requirements for endorsement accreditation?
- Have you identified key professional support staff within your institution who could advise you on course design? For example, this could be the careers service, student support services, learning developers or e-learning specialists.

Learning outcomes

Programme outcomes are the basis on which a course should be designed and getting them right from the outset will aid the development of a coherent course, with outcomes aligned at programme and module levels.

There will be a clear statement of outcomes for the whole programme and for each level within the programme specifications and these will reflect and be reflected by the learning outcomes within the component modules. Learning outcomes provide an indication to the level of a module and of the students' learning. Learning outcomes must be written in line with the QAA Framework for HE Qualifications and may also be informed by guidance from specialist bodies (e.g. SEEC, the Southern England Consortium for Credit Accumulation and Transfer, and NUCCAT, the Northern Universities Consortium for Credit Accumulation and Transfer).

Learning outcomes are pivotal to good course design because they help tutors clarify the learning objectives of the programme and the pathways within it. In addition they help to measure the programme objectives and intended standards against national benchmark standards. Learning outcomes also help students understand what they will gain from the programme and what they may expect of it and they help to determine learning strategies and forms of assessment.

Module learning outcomes are descriptors of what a student must know and be able to do in order to satisfy the requirements of a module and to gain credits. The learning outcome should be expressed in understandable language so as to avoid, as far as possible, misinterpretation (Gosling and Moon, 2001).

Three groups of outcome are generally identified in the programme and module specifications:

1. **Knowledge and understanding**. This means that after study the students should have a detailed knowledge base of the subject area, should be able to name major theories, relate their underlying principles and discuss the ideas, contexts and structures appropriate to the discipline. Students should be aware of ethical issues, and be able to debate the issues in the wider social, environmental and specific perspectives.

2. **Intellectual**. In this category students would be able to analyse, synthesize, evaluate and apply a range of information in the subject area. They should be able to select, compare, contrast and put into their own words a range of ideas, methods and techniques for gathering data in the discipline. Students should take increased responsibility for their own learning. They must be able to assess the worthiness of information and begin to recognize and find solutions to a range of issues with a considered approach.

3. **Practical/Professional Transferable skills**. In these categories students should begin to develop skills which will be useful to career development and potential employers. They should be able to work on their own, time manage effectively and also demonstrate the ability to work with others or on their own, to meet a deadline. Students should be able to use a range of communication tools to address a wide audience, for specific purposes, either professionally or personally.

> **Reflection point: what do the outcomes for your module look like?**
>
> - the standard module is likely to have 3–5 outcomes
> - the outcomes should derive from the programme outcomes but be adapted to show how the programme level outcome is reflected in that particular module
> - the outcomes should reflect a balance of the three categories
> - they must be measurable – assessment must cover all the learning outcomes
> - they should not contain evaluative words such as good, adequate, successful etc
> - they must be able to translate into assessment criteria (example in Appendix 5).

Employer engagement

Because Foundation Degrees are work-based, students may remain in work or have a placement within a work setting while they carry on with their study. This may mean that time spent in study has to be negotiated with the employer, facilitated during working hours or carried out in their own time with support and perhaps minimal attendance at the institution providing the award. Chapter 1 of this book discussed employer engagement as a unique feature of the Foundation Degree, as outlined in the Foundation Degree benchmark (QAA, 2010) and this chapter has already prompted reflection upon the role of employers as key stakeholders in the course design process. Therefore, it is important to note that a joint approach from academics and employers in shaping and influencing course content from inception, ensures that courses are as relevant as possible for employers.

> **Case study: engaging employers with course design**
>
> The FdA (Foundation Degree Arts) in Early Childhood Services at Bishop Grosseteste University College Lincoln was developed in 2006 to respond to the changing workforce development agenda of the then Labour government. The design of the Foundation Degree was based on experiences of academics who had been employed within early years care and education, and learning and teaching backgrounds, but the Foundation Degree also needed to show relevance to workforce development and employer engagement. Therefore the course was designed collaboratively by academics and members of the local authority-funded Early Years Development and Childcare Plan (EYDCP), in particular the officer responsible for
> ⇨

developing professional standards within early years nursery care and education. This was a small, but energetic team that met regularly and actively engaged with the design process and validation.

The practical management and organization of work-based learning should also be given consideration at the course design stage. It is important that the course team develop a shared vision not only of how they define work-based learning, but what it looks like in practice and what the role of employers may be in supporting learners within the workplace, for example, through mentoring. Mentoring in the workplace has always been a key issue and is determined by the position and interest attributed to the employer in contributing to, or the part played by him in assessment of the student. In many instances there is no requirement for employers to be part of the assessment process because the role is assumed by the HEI. If that is the case mentoring in the workplace should be supportive and negotiated, but ideally it should be underpinned by a learning agreement, signed by the employer and kept at the HEI (example in Appendix 4). In this way, roles and responsibilities are clearly indicated to the mentor and key contact in a separate sheet, and a member of the lecturing team is responsible for maintaining records and arranging visits to the setting where necessary. Mentors and key contacts should also have access to the virtual learning environment (VLE) at the HEI and be offered training in the role, alongside the student, so that all roles are clearly understood, manageable and equitable. Employer engagement is discussed further in Chapter 8.

Case study: partnership with the workplace

In one HEI, course staff are committed to visiting employment settings where Foundation Degree students are working or volunteering. Most of the visits take place early on in the first year, around the beginning of the second semester when students are established on the programme. This has become one of our signature practices and one that we now recognize as a tenet of the success of our programmes. The visits started as a reassuring presence for students and employers, but very quickly partners became more familiar with the HEI. By maintaining contact with an academic staff member, we found that the employer became more engaged with the academic programmes and understood the demands being made on the student. Face-to-face visits also provide opportunities for feedback and discussion between the HEI and employers especially with regard to the value of tasks and projects which are a crucial part of the design and assessment of Foundation Degrees and the progression routes.

Reflection point: employer engagement in practice

Making contact and arranging preliminary meetings can be the hardest stage of developing productive partnerships with employers, so think creatively about how you can do this! Be active in your pursuit of developing contacts – get out and meet employers, make telephone calls, be prepared to host meetings and enter into discussions. Most importantly, know what is available in the area so that you can identify gaps in provision for your area of expertise.

Learning and teaching strategies

A key part of the course design process relates to learning and teaching strategies, which should be devised to develop greater student independence and confidence in their learning process. It should be remembered that no one learning method or style will suit every student or every programme and that students should feel confident in the learning methods they use. Or put slightly differently, remember that the method or mode of teaching delivery is NOT the key to good learning – rather, ANY teaching method has the potential to be used in a way that makes learning possible. Kolb (1984) recognized that students or learners go through a cycle of learning and (as already outlined in Chapter 2) popularized the concept of the 'Experiential Learning Cycle' in a four-staged theory:

1. concrete experiences
2. observation and reflection
3. abstract conceptualization
4. testing concepts in new situations.

The learner passes through a process of experience, observation, reflection, formation and then testing. As they become comfortable with the subject content and more confident with their understanding, anxieties diminish and the learner tentatively, at first, tests out the new learning in existing work situations and then as confidence in abilities grows, begins to apply this understanding in new situations. The loop is continuous, building on experience and reflection; once the student's thinking is changed, information is assimilated, internalized and becomes embedded, the process begins again acting as a 'spiral of learning' continually building on reflections and actions.

To achieve satisfactory learning outcomes, students must have opportunities to test out their understanding; the ability to reflect, set personal targets and take action towards satisfying them, is a skill that needs to be practised. Students can be caught up in the assessment process as a means to an end and the inter-relationship between learning outcomes, learning opportunities and understanding can be blurred. However, for academics, it is the understanding of this relationship which should be paramount in the design of the degree.

In discussing approaches to learning and teaching, there are a whole range of methods of course delivery that could be considered. Many are

Table 4.1 Learning and teaching strategies

Mode of delivery	Issues for consideration
Lecture	Preparation time, delivery time, student engagement, space
Online strategies (see Chapter 6)	Preparation time, student engagement
Tutor-led seminar or workshop	Tutor-intensive if multiple tutors needed because of cohort size, space requirements
Tutor-facilitated activity (PBL, studio, stage, gym, lab work)	Clarity of tutor/student roles, specialist space requirements
Student-led seminar, workshop	Student preparation may be lacking
Guided reading (paper/web-based sources)	Students may need support in 'reading for information'
Student generated resources (video, posters, presentations)	Student preparation may be lacking, quality may be poor
Open access resources and shared resources	Sourcing and accessing relevant resources
Group tutorials	Tutor time, meeting space
Directed study/task	Clarity regarding where the task fits within the learning package. Space requirements
Peer teaching	Training and development for students
External speakers	Cost, assuring quality
Placement learning	Amount/type of tutor contact or facilitated time, use of e-tutorial support (e.g. webcam)
Field trips	Costs, supervision, timing
Work-based learning tasks	Student access to resources needed to complete tasks
Masterclasses	Specialist space requirements, 'expert' tutor/input needed

PBL, problem-based learning.

set out in Table 4.1, which may serve as a useful prompt for discussion within your teaching team.

Online strategies can be used as part of a blended approach to learning and teaching, but it must be clear where an online strategy may fit within the package of learning opportunities available to students. For example, an online strategy has the potential to:

- support student preparation for lectures and seminars
- aid directed study
- support tutor facilitation of individual tasks and group work (including asynchronous facilitation)
- promote study and communication skills (including independent learning and research skills).

To read more about e-learning, see Chapter 6.

Reflection point

The following questions may serve as useful prompts as you consider what learning and teaching strategies may be most appropriate for your course:
- What research evidence supports the choice of learning methods?
- Have a variety of learning methods been employed, including the use of learning technologies?
- Is the move to independence and autonomous learning staged and supported?
- In what ways do the proposed learning methods meet the diverse needs of the range of students, for example, mature, disabled or part-time?
- What are the resource implications of the chosen learning methods?

Case study: learning and teaching strategies

An integrated and interesting approach to Foundation Degree learning and teaching was needed for education and social care related courses in order to support students' academic study as well as sufficiently cater to disciplinary and professional specialisms. The majority of learners were mature students who, mostly, had little or no higher education experience, but what they did bring to their studies was work-based experience around the formal and informal education and care of children and young people. Therefore, a study skills module called 'Tools for Learning' became a cornerstone of the learning and teaching strategy. This module embedded study skills related to personal learning and the learning of children, thus integrating the twin demands of support for personal academic development for students within the context of a particular professional focus. ⇨

> Increasingly important was the need to develop and sustain interesting and engaging e-learning tasks, through our VLE. As designers, the use of e-learning in our 'blended-learning' strategy became paramount particularly as our students were on campus for face-to-face tuition only once a week, some travelling over 100 miles to be able to attend. The VLE became centrally embedded in our approach to learning and teaching – not to be used just as a repository for PowerPoint presentations, but as a powerful learning tool, designed to support individuals with their academic study. The VLE has become one of the most important factors for our Foundation Degree students in supporting student retention, improving accessibility to relevant resources and for supporting the completion of assessments.

Assessment strategies

Assessment is covered more fully in Chapter 7, but it is worth pausing here and considering the place of assessment within overall course design. Within programme documentation, it is usual for there to be a clear description of the assessment strategy and assessment methods within the rationale, with the assessment strategy also included in the programme specification (normally in tabular form). Of course, it is expected that there will be alignment between the overall programme-level strategy and individual assessment strategies in each module. In designing an effective assessment strategy, course teams should consider:

- the overall assessment load for students and the spread of assessment throughout the academic year
- the variety of assessment modes
- the comparability of student workload between all modules at the same level
- the relative comparability of loading for modules of different credit values
- the need to ensure all learning outcomes are assessed.

In addition, attention should be paid to the needs of students with disabilities in considering accessibility issues pertaining to the assessment strategy. At module level, course teams should consider the following:

- where an assessment is timed to occur within a module
- the mode of assessment
- how many assessment components are needed

- which learning outcomes a particular assessment may relate to
- the practicalities of assessment in terms of both student and tutor workload
- building in formative assessment opportunities without duplicating work for students and staff.

Module specifications

Module specifications form a core part of the programme documentation and experience has shown that work spent getting them right early on pays dividends in the long run. An exemplar pro forma can be found in Appendix 3. Normally, module specifications will contain information about learning hours, a rationale for the module, module learning outcomes, an outline of learning and teaching approaches, an indication of module content, assessment mode and weighting and an indicative reading list. It is worthwhile considering these aspects in turn, as each has a bearing upon overall course design.

Learning hours

Learning hours are the number of hours a student is expected to spend in study relating to a particular module or programme. The standard model is 10 hours for each credit point – in other words a 20-credit module should involve 200 learning hours. Learning hours tend to be made up of contact hours, directed study hours and independent learning hours. However, the notion of contact hours is highly contested in the FE and HE sector and this is an area that may warrant discussion within the course design team. It is important that you develop a shared view of what the term 'contact hours' means in the context of your course and there may be institutional guidance to take account of here too. For example, contact hours may include face-to-face contact with tutors (lecture, seminar, tutorial etc); online learning that involves engagement with tutors, including asynchronous learning; facilitated learning (problem-based learning, PBL) approaches, or work within a laboratory, studio, workshop, gym, stage or theatre with 'light-touch' facilitation by a tutor.

Directed study hours are less problematic as they tend to describe the time when the student goes away to complete a set task (e.g. specific preparation work for a session), whereas independent study hours indicate the time that a student is involved in directing their own learning.

Module rationale

Rationales outline why the module is being taught and its relationship to other modules at this and other levels. They should not be too long, but should contextualize the module within the wider programme to assure the reader that a coherent programme has been proposed.

Learning outcomes

Learning outcomes were discussed earlier in this chapter.

Module content

This section should include an indication of the proposed content for the module. Although content may be adjusted in the light of developments within the subject or work sector, indicative content helps to establish to students what is expected during the module.

Learning and teaching strategy

A short rationale should include the types of learning and teaching methods which you intend to adopt for the delivery of the programme. This may include a variety of pedagogical strategies, face-to-face whole class activity and the online environment. Traditional teaching methods such as seminars and workshops should be included as this will be familiar to students; the online discussion boards, wikis, and blogs will need support, to reduce anxiety and should be aligned to the concepts of contact time and learning hours.

Assessment

The basic requirements for module assessment information are:

- a short description of assessment types
- the weighting applied to each item of assessment
- possibly, an indication of the word count or equivalent, depending upon institutional policy in this area.

It is not necessary to include the actual title of the items of assessment unless they are specific to the outcomes of the module and will not change over time.

Case study: collaborative course design in practice

Intensive planning and development meetings are one way to manage course design activity. One course development exercise involved setting aside two full days in which key stakeholders were involved in the construction of a new Foundation Degree. Members of the programme team together with the head of department, the dean of school, the head of Learning and Teaching and colleagues from similar programmes engaged in open and robust discussion around course content, size and shape, with ideas recorded on laptops and whiteboards. An electronic shared area was used to lodge discussion content (e.g. this could be a shared computer drive or a web-based shared area such as SharePoint) and what emerged was a coherent structure, which the course team could use to further develop the detail of a new course. This is a perfect example of Belbin's (1993) principles for effective teamworking and collaborative practice: giving the team a set of objectives (content and design of degree) based around their individual experiences and professional knowledge (recognition and value), with each member of the team fulfilling a different function (a common purpose but different roles). This process took the whole day and raised many questions around academic level of study, the pros and cons of different credit amounts, assessment, and most crucially, whether this course would be acceptable to the HEI, our students and employers. At the end of the first day we had a design framework which could be circulated by email or lodged in the shared area for those who could not attend the development days due to working commitments. A prior telephone conversation with the programme team had taken place so the email was expected and they knew that a response was required immediately. Feedback was duly fed into the design the next day.

The second development day began with engaging in discussion with groups consisting of a mix of employers, tutors, senior management and past and current students, using the framework structure as a starting point. This consultation resulted in the programme team making subtle changes to the content, where appropriate. By the end of the day, we had reached a point where talk had given way to action – tutors were occupied with writing the first drafts of specific module specifications whereas others further developed the programme documentation in light of seeking sector endorsement. Working together we were able to support each other in constructing suitably levelled learning outcomes and in designing appropriate assessment tasks.

Progression routes

The successful completion of a Foundation Degree will provide 240 higher education credit points to the student and they will be entitled to use the letters FdA (Foundation Degree Arts) or FdSc (Foundation Degree Science) after their name. A distinct feature of Foundation Degrees is that they must also offer opportunities for progression to an honours degree award (QAA, 2010). In some cases the university validating the Foundation Degree will allow entry to relevant existing degrees in Year 3 (Level 6) or may design progression routes tailored specifically to offer the step up to a BA (Hons) degree. However, despite the expectation that progression routes will exist, there are some concerns about the lack of part-time articulation opportunities. In addition, Greenwood et al.'s (2008) study of early years and learning support Foundation Degree students noted that articulation routes were not timetabled to facilitate working patterns, making progression to honours degree study an inaccessible option for many. It is important, then, to give careful consideration to the provision of accessible progression routes for Foundation Degree graduates.

Case study: progression to honours level study

An association between Staffordshire University (as the validating HEI), Stoke-on-Trent College and British Telecom (BT) has resulted in a two-and-a-half year Foundation Degree programme during which time BT apprentices study and work. Following a one-semester 'bridging' course Foundation Degree graduates can continue their studies part-time to qualify as honours graduates in Computer Networks and Security.

Working with collaborative partners

Collaborative partnerships can be formed when the HEI, the FE College, the training agency or an employer has made contact to discuss the opportunities available. Reasons for this could be where popular demand for skills related to a sector specialism have been identified, and/or where there is a shortfall in provision or when employers wish their own training courses to be accredited. The process of validation has to be undertaken to ensure the quality and levelness of the programme and provision. This process can be entered into using the advice and guidance mentioned earlier in the chapter. It is slightly less complicated when FE colleges (FEC) adopt a previously accredited and validated course from an established HEI. The FEC demonstrates that they are equipped with suitable resources to deliver the programme to meet the HEI's Quality Assurance practices.

Areas for consideration to develop partnership agreements are: Programme resources:

- staff qualifications and staff development
- programme leadership
- library resources at HE Levels 4 and 5
- e-learning resources and support
- dedicated teaching areas
- student numbers.

Quality Assurance issues:

- Code of Practice for Collaborative Provision (satisfied that all the above bullet points are addressed)
- the committee structure (monitoring quality)
- the link tutor role (monitoring resources)
- student intake (potential impact on student numbers for progression routes).

Case study

A local FE college has identified growing need in a sector and approaches the HEI delivering a similar programme which also offers a progression route from the FdA. The HEI satisfactorily completes preliminary investigations and senior members of staff from the HEI and FEC meet to discuss the programme – documents may be shared at this point and the FEC programme team develop their documentation to meet the points raised above. A member of staff (this may be a link tutor) from the HEI is identified and will be the main point of contact for the FEC staff during this development period. At a previously arranged time the HEI (quality team), link tutor, external academic with expertise in the sector and FEC staff will meet at the validation panel where the documents will be scrutinized. The FEC would normally host the proceedings arranging for the visiting panel to have had sight of the documentation and to be given a tour of resources to satisfy the Quality Assurance of the programme and facilities.

From the HEI's perspective it is assumed that students attending courses delivered at the FECs should have an equitable experience to that of those offered at the HEI especially when progression routes are offered at the HEI from the Foundation Degrees.

Summary

This chapter has explored the process of Foundation Degree course design from the very first steps in identifying ideas for courses, through the planning and approval process. It is important to recognize that the hard work put in early on to the planning and design process should reap dividends later in the form of a course that is coherent, well-designed, fit for the purpose, interesting to students and acceptable to employers. Many aspects of Foundation Degree delivery that have been touched upon in this chapter are explored in more detail in later chapters – for example in relation to learning, teaching and assessment. In addition, guidance has been given regarding the nature of employer engagement.

References

Belbin, R. (1993), *Team Roles at Work.* Oxford: Butterworth Heinemann.

Biggs, J. (1999), *Teaching for Quality Learning at University.* Buckingham, UK: Open University Press.

Gosling, D. and Moon, J. (2001), *How to Use Learning Outcomes and Assessment Criteria.* London: SEEC.

Greenwood, M., Little, B. with Burch, E., Collins, C., Kimura, M. and Yarrow, K. (2008), *Report to Foundation Degree Forward on the Impact of Foundation Degrees on Students and the Workplace.* London: Centre for Higher Education Research and Information,The

Open University and the Learning and Skills Network. Available online at: www.fdf.ac.uk/downloads/11/20090806172043fdf_research_summary.pdf (accessed 15 March 2011).

Kolb, D. A. (1984), *On Experiential Learning*. Available online at: www.infed.org/biblio/b-explrn.htm (accessed 15 March 2011).

QAA (2006), 'Programme design, approval, monitoring and review', *Code of Practice for the Assurance of Academic Quality and Standards in Higher Education*. Available online at: www.qaa.ac.uk/Publications/InformationAndGuidance/Pages/Code-of-practice-section-7.aspx (accessed 30 August 2011).

— (2010), *Foundation Degree Qualification Benchmark*. Gloucester: QAA.

Walsh, A. (2007), 'An exploration of Biggs' constructive alignment in the context of work-based learning', *Assessment and Evaluation in Higher Education*, 32 (1), 79–87.

5 Teaching Strategies

Sacha Mason

This chapter will:

- explore the range of teaching strategies which can be successfully implemented in a Foundation Degree programme
- identify the needs of work-based learners
- discuss the strength of the learning community for work-based learners
- focus on the blended learning approach that typically incorporates face-to-face, facilitated and independent and workplace learning.

The process of organizing teaching is really about designing learning (D'Andrea, 2003, p. 26), and is an important consideration when meeting the learning needs of all students, particularly those studying in Foundation Degrees. The specific characteristics of Foundation Degree students, identified in Chapter 3, require particular examination when designing programmes of learning. For Foundation Degree students, the return to formal learning may represent a life change, an opportunity for career progression, or a personal goal, and as such Foundation Degree students come to HE with high expectations of themselves and with considerable commitment to their learning. This translates into levels of motivation which Walkin (1990) suggests are the keystones to learning. These levels of motivation potentially place the lecturer in a privileged position in teaching a group of highly motivated learners. However, although motivated, the diverse range of entry qualifications that students have already acquired, along with the broad profile identified in Chapter 3, frequently requires carefully designed Foundation Degree programmes that provide the underpinning study skills to enable them to meet the demands of learning at HE levels. Embedded within the programme should be strategies that support independent and autonomous learning, a key feature of learning at the HE level. The transition from dependent to independent learning should be gradually and strategically built into teaching strategies, beginning from the first module of the programme. This transition requires careful management with Foundation Degree students as, for many, the return to formal education can be highly stressful. Work-based students manage many demands on their time and this can generate much anxiety. A progressive building of content, underpinned with study skills supports student confidence and development. Investment in establishing study skills as part of, and linked to, the programme content is time well spent as students begin to develop their research/writing/communication skills. These can be suitably supported through access to Learning Developers as well as to lecturers, and most importantly to the learning community (see Chapter 3).

Reflection point

The challenge for many HE institutions delivering work-based degrees is in managing and supporting the wide range of student competencies that are characteristic of Foundation Degree learners. Consider what strategies can be implemented by you and your teaching team to support the development of these students, such as embedding study skills into modules, study skills workshops, or the focused use of 'learning developers' referred to in Chapter 3.

The learning community

The term 'learning community' refers to learning activities that are generated as part of student engagement with their course such as teacher and student/students context and student-led activities. A feature of a learning community is that learning takes place within a social learning dimension and the concept of Vygotsky's social learning theory is relevant here. The understanding that learning is a social activity, both through scaffolded interactions and the Zone of Proximal Development (ZPD) (Vygotsky, 1978, p. 86), enables a pedagogy to develop that is shaped by a learning community. Lave (2009, p. 201) provides a current perspective on the theories of Vygotsky to describe 'situated activity' which involves changes in knowledge and action, and therefore describes learning. Situated activity denotes the context that the learner is in and their participation in a process of 'changing and understanding practice'. Students on a Foundation Degree are work-based learners in varied settings and as such are learners engaged in their own 'situated learning', an idea explored in Chapter 2. This additional dimension, or learning community of the workplace, requires a pedagogy that is responsive to the individual nature of the range of 'situated learning' that the students encounter; the workplace and the HE institution, and indeed others. An appropriate pedagogical approach for these students is for the programme content, for example theoretical models, to be contextualized, through both individual and/or group scaffolding, to their work-based experiences. These links to practice can be made during teaching sessions through frequent and explicit use of experiences to a wider application from either the lecturer or indeed their fellow students and as such, learning is an active and collective process. The concepts are made even more meaningful when students return to their workplace and are able to reflect on their learning and make the theoretical links to their practice for themselves. As Lave (2009, p. 203) suggests:

> Acquisition of knowledge is not a simple matter of taking in knowledge; rather, things assumed to be natural categories, such as 'bodies of knowledge', 'learners', and 'cultural transmission', require reconceptualisation as cultural, social products.

The application of knowledge to enable understanding, and as such learning, is situational and the contextual needs of the learner require close consideration to enable the 'reconceptualisation' of new knowledge; the teacher needs to know their students. The contextual needs along with the needs of the learner are dependent on the relationships between the pedagogue and the learning community. Social learning occurs through sensitive and trusting relationships that are intuitive to the learning and the learners. Petty (1998, p. 15) refers to the features or needs of learning in the mnemonic 'educare?':

E – Explanation

The students need to understand why the skill is carried out in the way it is, along with any important background information.

D – Doing-detail

The students must discover precisely what they are expected to do, and how it should be done. This is the 'doing-detail' which students often best learn by being 'shown-how' for example, via a demonstration or a case study. These provide models of good practice to copy or adapt, and are useful precisely because they provide the 'doing-detail'.

U – Use

The students must use – that is, practise – the skill.

C – Check and correct

Students' practice must of course be checked and corrected by the students themselves, and usually by the teacher.

A – Aide-memoire

The students need some reminder or other – for example notes, handout, book, tape etc.

R – Review

And reuse of earlier work is required to ensure that old learning is not forgotten.

E – Evaluation

Learning must be tested under realistic conditions, if the learner and the teacher are to be confident of the learning.

? – Queries

Learners always require an opportunity to ask questions.

(Petty, 1998, p. 15)

The features of learners identified in E,D,U, Evaluation and Queries are related to the learning community and the connections that work-based students can make within their cohort and beyond, within their working environments. Specific provision should be made to develop the sense of community for the students through access to resources and strategies that encourage communication between students and staff which is especially relevant when students are only on-site for a limited time. A virtual learning environment (VLE), or e-learning resources, can provide these opportunities and support the development of a learning community and this is discussed further in Chapter 6. The value of a learning community for all types of students is essential, and has particular resonance for work-based learners.

Learner-focused strategies

The features of learning that Petty (1998) outlines have relevance in the discussion of appropriate teaching strategies on Foundation Degrees. The importance of learning relationships is pertinent from the positions of 'teacher-focused' and 'learner-focussed' education. A learner-focused approach identifies the individual nature of learning: that the process of learning and indeed the outcome of the learning is highly individualized. Jarvis (2009, p. 24) suggests 'it is the person who learns and it is the changed person who is the outcome of the learning, although that changed person may cause several different social outcomes'. Light and Cox (2001, p. 46) extend the 'learner focussed' approach and suggest that 'learning is not entirely or even mostly in the power of the teacher', making planning for learning in a higher education context, challenging and complex. The fundamental shift in 'power' (Light and Cox, 2001) of the learning to the learner may position the teacher in an alternative role and framework; one that challenges the traditional didactic approach to teaching in higher education and suggests the exploration of a more dialogic approach, interaction rather than transmission. It is these alternative views of the nature of teaching and learning that are explored in this chapter. In locating the function of the teacher within Foundation Degree programmes, the relationship between the active learning of students and the reflective teacher becomes evident in teasing out the paradigms of teacher and learner. It is necessary to acknowledge the complexities of the two concepts and their inter-relationship.

Teaching strategies

The 'educare?' (Petty, 1998, p. 15) mnemonic outlines the needs of the students in relation to the learning of skills although it does not outline specific teaching strategies. The notion of a specific or fixed pedagogy may not be helpful as the idea of a prescribed set of teaching strategies may not suit the institution, teacher or indeed the students. As such a flexible approach by the teacher may be required to respond to the diverse and individual learning needs. However, suggestions for teaching strategies are made in this chapter which have been implemented on a Foundation Degree and are discussed to provide a starting point or initial framework. Reference to the 'teacher' depicts the person who leads learning.

The term 'active learning', according to Bonwell and Eison (1991, p. 2), describes the process of engagement in reading, writing, solving problems and other higher-order thinking such as analysis, synthesis and evaluation, through 'doing things and thinking about what they [the learner] are doing'. However, Mayer (2004) suggests that a distinction should be made between Bronwell and Eison's definition of 'active', which denotes behavioural activity, and cognitive activity. Cognitive activity may not necessarily involve 'doing'. Bronwell and Eison (1991) do suggest that ways in which learning may be active depends on the learning style, or the approach to learning, of the individual and the deployment of a combination of teaching strategies may be considered to be the most appropriate pedagogical approach to maximize the learning opportunities for students. The diverse combination of teaching strategies that

Table 5.1 Blended learning on a Foundation Degree

Face-to-face	Facilitated and independent	Workplace
Large groups	Self-directed	Directed tasks
Small groups	Peer-supported	
Tutorials	Virtual learning environment (VLE)	
	Problem-based learning (PBL)	

can be encompassed on a Foundation Degree (Table 5.1) are largely established through a blended learning approach: face-to-face contact time usually at a formal learning institution, facilitated and independent learning and learning situated in the work setting. The richness of the blended approach enables students to engage with aspects of these strategies that assist in their deep learning. Atherton (2009) summarizes some of the approaches that are features of 'deep learning', which include the ability to relate previous knowledge to new knowledge, to focus on what is 'signified', to relate theoretical ideas to everyday experiences, to organize and structure content into a coherent whole where the emphasis is internal, from within the student, and to relate and distinguish evidence and argument. Atherton's model has similarities with Petty's features for learning and as such should be encompassed for deep learning to be an outcome of an Foundation Degree programme.

Face-to-face learning

The face-to-face contact time with students on a work-based degree is often significantly reduced in comparison with traditional undergraduate degrees. Contact time may be during evening hours one day a week, a series of evenings a week, weekends or one day in the week. This contact time can be used in different ways, large and small groups and one-to-one contact which each have their value and relevance within a Foundation Degree programme.

Large group

Large group teaching can be demanding for students to follow and recent research (Mason, 2009) suggests that a more valued version of the traditional didactic lecture is the interactive lecture. The distinction between a conventional, didactic, exposition style of lecture, is in contrast to an interactive lecture that invites comments and discussion from students both formally and informally. Collins et al. (2002, p. 1) comment that they 'hold in esteem a learning process that is active and interactive, set within the context of warm and nurturing relationships and rich in communication'. The notion of 'warm and nurturing relationships' is critical as the personality of the teacher determines the type of relationship established between student and teacher. The interactive elements require the teacher to be flexible and confident in their management of the group to allow for spontaneous, whole class discussion to take place, along with a secure content knowledge.

Learner voice

Research evidence (Mason, 2009) suggests the rich learning opportunities afforded through the interactive lecture.

'Interactive elements [in lectures] helps you to clarify what you think.' (Foundation Degree Student, Year 2)

'The lecture plants the seeds and the discussion gives it more dimension.' (Foundation Degree Student, Year 2)

'I think sometimes, certain things you say [teacher] will really trigger something in your own life, something specific to you [the student].' (Foundation Degree Student, Year 2)

'extending our thinking, 'cos, you know, we will say comments and you [me as the teacher] will extend that and say "Why do you think that?" and it really makes us think and everyone having the chance to say what they think, and listening to each others' views.' (Foundation Degree, Year 1)

'we can bounce the ideas off from each other and learn from each other as well rather than just being given information.' (Foundation Degree, Year 1)

Mason (2009) found that the students referred to, when a 'very academic' lecture had been delivered to the group, and reported feeling overwhelmed by the density of the content of the lecture and the didactic approach. This teaching strategy had not enabled a warm and discursive relationship to be developed and the students spoke of feeling out of their depth with the lecture content. This suggests that a flexible dialogic approach is required to check the learning and understanding of the students at regular points. An interactive approach allows for Explanation, Review and Evaluation (Petty's mnemonic 1998, p. 15) to be undertaken, that is, the linking of theoretical concepts to practice and to previous knowledge and to 'Check and Correct' learning. The most important of the students' needs, that of queries and questions, can also be provided for with this strategy. The students refer to the ability to 'think' in interactive lectures, rather than being overwhelmed with information. Mayer (2004) suggests that cognitive activity may not necessarily involve 'doing'. The notion of 'doing' refers to behavioural activity in the context of discovery learning. In an interactive lecture, students may not be engaged in a behaviourally active, independent, problem solving task but are still 'doing' thinking.

Teaching resources in a whole class session are also of importance. A common resource that is frequently used is the PowerPoint presentation. Mann and Robinson (2009) refer to PowerPoint presentations, from the findings of a survey of 211 students from a university in the north-west of England, as being a key reason for the boredom rates of students. The use of PowerPoint slides can be a factor for, and also an obstacle for preventing, learning. Where PowerPoint slides do not correlate with the teacher's exposition, students may become distracted. The value of PowerPoint is that it may serve as a visual prompt for students in making sense of the content during the lecture, keeping track while taking notes and as an aide-memoire (Petty's mnemonic 1998, p.15) for assessments. When slides are overloaded with text or not in a linear sequence in relation to the presenters' exposition, then students may become distracted or confused. The use of pictures are of particular value when carefully chosen and relevant, although they may equally present challenges to learning when not immediately accessible to students. The specific time constraints of Foundation Degree students due to relatively limited contact time require that resources are quickly accessible and have value beyond the classroom to the student. This may be in providing references within PowerPoint slides when lecturers use quotations for handouts to become a useful resource for assessments and further research. Likewise, notes made during lectures on the slide handouts provide an essential part of effective learning. Petty (1998) outlines the difficulties that students have in note taking, particularly in relation to writing and listening simultaneously. The inter-relationship between the slide handout and student note taking is relevant; where students are presented with content that is structured and summarized into bullet points in a presentation, it may assist further learning through the linear note taking opportunities for students. Content may also be supported through the careful selection of directed reading for students to be undertaken prior to the taught session, where specific excerpts or chapters from relevant texts are made available through the VLE. This assists the students in familiarizing with the session content prior to attending on-site classes.

Small group

The use of small group discussion and activities has particular value on a work-based degree. The diverse employment experiences that Foundation Degree students bring to discussions make a rich source of knowledge and understanding available to the learning community. Opportunities to access and capitalize on these sources enables students to develop their learning beyond their own employment setting. Small group discussion is a significant feature of work-based Foundation Degrees where 'learning is seen as participation in the social world' (Taylor, 2008, p. 54).

Case study: using discussion groups in learning and teaching

Students on a Foundation Degree in Children's Services for employees working with children from 0 to 19 years are able to develop their understanding of the issues within the wider sector, through small discussion groups. For example, a student working within the early years has the opportunity to discuss inter-agency working within the *Every Child Matters* agenda (2003) with a fellow student working within the youth work sector. The discussion provides chances for practice comparisons to be made and for an appreciation of the issues related to different ages and stages of children. In turn, less experienced practitioners may have access to more experienced colleagues to share best practices.

The design of small group work can enrich the opportunities for sharing practice experiences within the learning community through a variety of different groups such as friendship groups, employment sector pathway groups, cross-sector pathway groups, diverse groups where students do not know each other or in pairs, and this facilitates learning during the course of the programme. David (2010) suggests that an effective strategy for teaching a work-based degree includes drawing on personal experiences which places value on experiential prior learning. However, some students may express initial discomfort with or reluctance to work in unfamiliar groups but, after the initial reluctance, usually find the diversity of views to be a strength. Reluctance to engage with wider groups beyond friendship groups can be attributed to a lack of confidence. Careful management of groups is necessary in developing student confidence. A characteristic of work-based students is that they are often more mature students and therefore may view the teacher as too 'autocratic' (Exley and Dennick 2004, p. 36) if always directed to designated groups, and as such some students' learning may be compromised resulting in disengagement from the programme. This tension can be addressed by a range of strategies that the teacher employs to form a variety of groups: some student nominated groups and some teacher-led. Exley and Dennick (2004, p. 37) refer to the work of Heron (1989) who concludes that:

> the most effective facilitator [teacher] attitude should value autonomy, co-operation and hierarchy in that order as this recognises the personal autonomy of group members to self-actualize in collaboration with others with the facilitator taking responsibility to achieve the group goals.

The necessity for the teacher to take responsibility to achieve the group goals is critical in outcome-driven programmes such as Foundation Degrees, but requires some flexibility in how these are achieved.

Walklin (1990) refers to facilitative teaching which is student-led or learner-focused and which requires a high level of participation where students accept considerable responsibility for their own learning outcomes. This is necessary in small group work where students are required to undertake a problem-based activity. The issues for the teacher in employing strategies that are student-led require the teacher to relinquish some control over the learning that takes place, while ensuring opportunities to learn. Possible limitations of any small group work are that the students do not remain focused on the task, are dominated by one member that restricts contributions from others or that outcomes are not met. The arrangement of groups can address some of these limitations by ensuring that group participants are logistically able to make eye contact through organization of the physical space, that less confident group members are given the chance to assume a more dominant role and that provision is made for students to feedback their outcomes to the whole class following the group session. These arrangements assist in minimizing some of the limitations of group work, although the role of the teacher is an essential aspect in providing a group task that is clear and relevant, checking progress to ensure that groups are able to manage the task and also to know when to intervene or support a group. The latter form of assistance is the most challenging as frequent disruption by the teacher can inhibit group action and discussion.

Reflection point

The use of written, audio or filmed case studies where groups are required to respond to the problem posed or to critique the case is a valuable tool for work-based learners. A relevant case study allows students to explore the issues related to their employment sector, apply theoretical frameworks and engage in analytical discussion. The tutor can strategically pose questions that stimulate discussion or enhance the case at opportune moments during the session which enables some control over the learning outcomes. A feedback session at the end of the group work, allows the teacher to check learning and to develop a wider discussion with the whole class. How could you source or develop relevant case study material for use with your Foundation Degree students?

Tutorials

David (2010, p. 186) uses the term 'learning transition' in describing the adjustment that students are required to make from previous learning experiences and their working environment to that of learning at HE levels and expectations. This learning transition can be observed in all students but particularly so in Foundation Degree students as they are enculturated into learning at university (David, 2010, p. 186). All the teaching strategies discussed require consideration as part of the student learning transition, although the use of tutorials can enhance the learning transition, or indeed inhibit it. Tutorials are typically undertaken with the teacher on a one-to-one basis and they provide the opportunity for the student to individually discuss their learning and therefore, can enable differentiated support by the teacher. Factors that contribute to the success of tutorials rely on the student/teacher relationship. David (2010) refers to research that indicates some aspects of academic writing that work-based learners specifically find difficult and lack confidence which requires considerable support from teachers. Tutorials provide the opportunity to address concerns about academic writing with the student and to signpost students to the wider support, such as learning advice, available for them to access. The issue of student confidence is important as it may inhibit learning and motivation. David (2010) outlines the need for teachers to connect with students' lives in order to support their learning and wider development. Tutorials provide the time to engage with the student's wider experiences that contribute to their levels of learning. Effective interpersonal communication is necessary to adopt a more holistic approach to the student. The view of the student as a whole may be challenging for some teachers who perceive that their role is to only support the student on matters of their learning. However, the different roles of employee/parent/spouse/student means that for Foundation Degree students it is important to view them in their wider context, as the roles beyond that of the student may affect their learning. Walklin (1990, p. 196) suggests that barriers to communication can be extrinsic and intrinsic. Extrinsic barriers include noise levels and the environment in general. Intrinsic barriers may be based on past experiences, feelings and 'internal thought processes relating to both the communicator, and message content'. The past and wider experiences of the student, therefore, should be taken into account to assist the student's learning.

Reflection point

Tutorials are demanding for the tutor when required for large cohorts of students. Consider these strategies for managing the tutorial process:

- ensuring the student arrives prepared with questions for discussion
- read drafts of the student's work prior to the tutorial to enable a focused discussion
- provide a tutorial room that minimizes disruption and noise

- ensure students arrive promptly and are aware of the time slot they have been allocated
- be realistic about the amount of time spent with each student and keep to time
- be prepared to offer more support at another designated time if unexpected support is required.

Facilitated and independent learning

The second strand of blended learning embodies a range of strategies and tools that enable Foundation Degree students to be supported in their learning by the teacher although it does not require face-to-face, or on-site, access. Typically these strategies support self-directed, peer-supported and problem-based learning. A key tool in this strand is the use of the wealth of e-learning resources such as a VLE.

Virtual learning environment

The blended learning approach incorporates strategies to support learning when the student is not attending taught sessions on-site at the HEI. Blended learning, that depicts e-learning, workplace learning and more traditional on-site learning, is a characteristic of Foundation Degrees.

The VLE is a valuable resource for students' learning. The ability to access programme resources and materials when off site promotes student independence and enables the continued sense of being part of a learning community. The learning community, according to Collins et al. (2002, p. 132), is established on the premise that 'learning is social and that communication and relationship are at the heart of good learning'. Starratt (1996) refers to three main characteristics of a learning community:

1. a critical community of inquirers who share understandings
2. the learning agenda explores questions important to individuals
3. learning is related to students' everyday lives.

The community is enhanced from the students' shared appreciation of the challenges facing work-based learners such as employment, family and study responsibilities which are characteristic of Foundation Degree students. On reflection, the establishment of learning communities is essential for all aspects of learning such as learning how to learn and the practicalities of learning with the programme content. Indeed Senge et al. (1994) refer to learning communities as 'deep learning cycles'. The connections with the learning community can be continued when away from the HEI through interactive elements on the VLE such as the online journal, the blog and the Wiki. These facilities provide a learning tool for reflection, for communication and serve as a central repository of information and research that is accessible both on and off site. Where these interactive elements can provide a supportive network is in the opportunity to address practical or logistical issues of their learning together which raises confidence through mutual support and creates an effective learning community. e-Learning is explored in more detail in Chapter 6.

Learning resources

Learning resources, in this instance, refer to the resources that are available to students to support their wider, independent learning. These resources may be many. For instance, with more formal learning such as that undertaken on a degree programme they may be library resources such as books, journals and other publications. The learning resource of time can be included in this regard, time to study and complete assignments. Time constraints are an important factor for students studying in work-based degrees with the many demands on their time. Accessibility of resources for learning is therefore a key factor for successful learning. Student perceptions of libraries (Mason, 2009) suggest that the categorization of books, in some libraries, makes for a frustrating search for relevant texts. The idiosyncratic categorization of books in university libraries becomes an aspect of the enculturation of learning at HE level and can be therefore exclusive of some students. The limited time spent on-site when the library is available means that time spent seeking books, which then require further research to elicit the required information, can be challenging. Induction into the use of the library can provide students with the knowledge of the process of finding books and scanned excerpts from texts on the VLE can assist with the direct access, for students, of relevant texts appropriate to the programme. David (2010, p. 196) refers to Hockings et al. (2010) in describing an appropriately inclusive pedagogy that uses 'resources, materials, humour, examples, and anecdotes that are sensitive to the social and cultural diversity of the group'. The sensitive use of resources, and access to them, is critical in empowering work-based degree students to learn through the creation of conditions to make learning possible.

Learning in the workplace

The third strand of the blended learning approach encompasses the learning that occurs within the work setting. The content of the programme needs to have direct relevance to the work setting and incorporate elements where students can apply their knowledge and experience. Petty's mnemonic (1998, p. 15) draws together the features or needs of learning and identifies the aspects of learning that are supported by the workplace. The 'use' feature links to the workplace where students are able to be actively engaged in using the knowledge and understanding that they have learnt from the other strands of blended learning.

Case study: work-based learning in action

Students are undertaking a research project as part of a module on an FdA in Children's Services. The focus of the project is practitioner research methodology and students are required to form recommendations for developing their practice as part of the research process. Sally has chosen to focus on the value of outdoor play in her early years setting as part of her research project. She has undertaken some data collection which has involved listening to the voices of children and this has elicited some findings that have allowed Sally to question the layout of the outdoor provision. Sally has acted on these findings and continued to monitor the views of the children and staff as to the effectiveness of the setting's provision.

The process of learning research skills and the opportunity to undertake a small-scale project allowed Sally to reflect on her learning undertaken as part of her degree programme. Evaluation (Petty, 1998, p. 15) is seen as a further feature of learning and is enabled through the 'testing' of learning under realistic conditions. The research project in this example provided opportunity to 'test', question and explore knowledge and understanding and, as outlined in Chapter 2, the workplace has provided the forum for learning. In Sally's example, her learning has been more formally structured through the assessment process and the undertaking of a research project as part of the programme. In addition to these more formally designed opportunities, students on a Foundation Degree may also engage in informal learning within the workplace. Informal learning is through using the skills they acquire in the process of undertaking a degree in higher education such as high order cognitive functions. David (2010) advocates a pedagogy that is flexible and enables student-centred activity which allows for the application of their own knowledge and experience, which needs to be at the heart of a work-based degree programme. It is important to acknowledge the valuable contribution that students may make to the programme in terms of the knowledge and experiences that they bring. Listening to students and hearing their voice in relation to sector-specific knowledge can ensure the programme content retains currency.

Case study: valuing students' workplace experience

John is a lecturer on an FdA in Administration Management and identifies the value in listening to students in relation to keeping his own knowledge current.

One of the key aspects of the programme, for me, is when a student suggests a new method for managing information that they are trialling within their work placement which offers a different way of operating, for example new computer software or product. The student's workplace experiences help me to keep abreast of changes within the sector or working environment and alerts me to the pressures that differing employers are facing. This is vital to support the currency of the programme along with adding validity and importance to this strand of the blended learning pedagogy. I find that the more I utilize students' workplace experience, the more confident the student is in making the links between the strands of blended learning. The workplace environment is the most familiar to the student and it is where they often feel the most confident and through valuing this strand of learning, I feel that the student feels that they have something important to contribute to their learning community and workplace.

John's acknowledgement that he is able to use his students' experiences and workplace knowledge to enhance his own is a powerful pedagogical tool and a critical feature of a Foundation Degree. Ivanic and Lea (2006, p. 8) suggest that traditionally universities have been seen as the 'bastions of academic knowledge' however, with the changing landscape of HE and the introduction of work-based, vocationally orientated courses, this raises questions of universities as the 'knowledge-holders' and 'knowledge-providers' (an idea explored in Chapter 2) and perhaps suggests a more shared, collaborative approach with each participant, teacher and student having a valuable contribution to make.

Summary

This chapter has sought to explore the pedagogical approaches that can be used for a Foundation Degree programme. It has explored the blended learning strands and offered a rationale for developing them as part of a work-based programme. However, although the suggested strategies have been tried and tested you should not be limited to just those addressed in this chapter. A diverse perspective on pedagogies should be maintained and this can be supported through consultation with students. Frequently, students have a clear understanding of how they learn best or more importantly knowledge of the strategies and conditions where they do not learn and, therefore, it is essential to seek the views of students to support pedagogical change. Furthermore David (2010, p. 201) calls for personal pedagogies that ensure 'people's lives across the life course' are enhanced and improved. The motivation for a student to undertake a Foundation Degree may be linked to a desire for career progression or a personal goal and as such it is important that an appropriate pedagogy is adopted that can support individual enhancement and improvement.

References

Atherton, J. (2009), *Learning and Teaching: Deep and Surface Learning*. Available online at: www.learningandteaching.info/learning/deepsurf.htm (accessed 23 September 2010).

Bonwell, C. and Eison, J. (1991), 'Active Learning – Creating Excitement in the Classroom'. AEHE – ERIC. Higher Education Report No.1. Washington DC: Jossey-Bass.

Collins, J., Harkin, J. and Nind, M. (2002), *Manifesto for Learning*. London: Continuum.

D'Andrea, V. (2003), 'Organizing teaching and learning: outcomes-based planning', in Fry, H., Ketteridge, S. and Marshall, S. (eds), *A Handbook for Teaching and Learning in Higher Education*. (2nd edn). Oxon: RoutledgeFalmer.

David, M. (ed.) (2010), *Improving Learning by Widening Participation in Higher Education*. London: Routledge.

DfES (2003), *Every Child Matters*. Available online at: www.education.gov.uk/publications/standard/publicationdetail/page1/CM5860 (accessed 13 April 2011).

Exley, K. and Dennick, R. (2004), *Small Group Teaching: Tutorials, Seminars and Beyond*. London: Routledge.

Heron, J. (1989), *Approaches to Small Group Learning and Teaching*. University of Glasgow.

Hockings, C., Cooke, S., Yamashita, H., McGinty, S. and Bowl, M. (2009), 'Learning and teaching in two different universities within the context of increasing student diversity – complexity, contradiction and challenge', in David, M. (ed.), *Improving Learning by Widening Participation to Higher Education*. London: Routledge.

Ivanic, R. and Lea, M. (2006), 'New contexts, new challenges: the teaching of writing in UK Higher Education', in Ganobcsik-Williams, L. (ed.), *Teaching Academic Writing in UK Higher Education*. Hampshire: Palgrave Macmillan.

Jarvis, P. (2009), 'Learning to be a person in society: learning to be me', in Illeris, K. (ed.), *Contemporary Theories: Learning Theorists. . .in Their Own Words*. Oxon: Routledge.

Lave, J. (2009), 'The practice of learning', in Illeris, K. (ed.), *Contemporary Theories: Learning Theorists. . .in Their Own Words*. Oxon: Routledge.

Light, G. and Cox, R. (2001), *Learning and Teaching in Higher Education: The Reflective Professional*. London: PCP.

Mann, S. and Robinson, A. (2009), 'Boredom in the lecture theatre: an investigation into the contributors, moderators and outcomes of boredom amongst university students', *British Educational Research Journal*, 35 (2), 243–258.

Mason, S. (2009) 'Impact research project conducted for postgraduate certificate of professional studies in education'. Unpublished. Bishop Grosseteste University College.

Mayer, R. (2004), 'Should there be a three-strikes rule against pure discovery learning? The case for guided methods of instruction', *American Psychologist*, 59 (1), 14–19.

Petty, G. (1998), *Teaching Today*. Cheltenham: Nelson Thornes.

Senge, P., Kleiner, A., Roberts, C., Ross, R. and Smith, B. (1994), *The Fifth Discipline Field Book: Strategies and Tools for Building a Learning Organisation*. New York: Currency Doubleday.

Starratt, R. (1996), *Transforming Educational Administration: Meaning Community and Excellence*. New York: McGraw-Hill.

Taylor, C. (2008), 'Legitimising Foundation Degrees: principles, practice and pedagogy', *Educational Futures*, 1 (1), 47–59. Available online at:
www.educationstudies.org.uk/materials/taylor2.pdf (accessed 30 August 2011).

Vygotsky, L. (1978), *Mind in Society: The Development of Higher Psychological Processes*. London: Harvard University Press.

Walkin, L. (1990), *Teaching and Learning in Further and Adult Education*. Cheltenham: Nelson Thomas.

e-Learning 6
David Barber

Chapter Outline

This chapter will:

- explore why e-learning is relevant to Foundation Degrees
- look at ways in which learning technologies support employer engagement
- define the virtual learning environment (VLE) and the educational importance of the World Wide Web
- look at ways in which the learning environment supports students
- explore the pedagogical basis for the use of learning technologies.

Introduction

It has already been noted that the QAA defines the Foundation Degree as 'a collaboration between employers and programme providers' (QAA, 2010, p. 4). We might, therefore, reasonably expect technology to play an important role in Foundation Degree programmes as it is an important feature of both educational and professional environments.

Most importantly we might hope to use it to overcome some of the very significant challenges that arise from the divide that exists between the worlds of work and learning. For the Foundation Degree learner, this divide involves practical issues arising from differences in physical location and in this respect certain technologies – notably email – have found a role in facilitating communication across these barriers. However, the divide also operates at a conceptual level, for working and learning environments are often characterized by different values, standards and practices.

Given these differences effective collaboration depends on both parties understanding each other's role as well as the nature of their own commitment, which must be meaningful and have a clear relationship to positive outcomes. From the employer's perspective, confidence relies ultimately on the perception that the programme provider is acting in good faith in seeking to understand their needs and to reflect those needs in the structure and content of the Foundation Degree. To make a meaningful contribution technology ought to try and address all these issues and, although email is convenient and cost-effective, we might question whether it can, on its own, meet the full range of requirements raised by such collaboration.

Document sharing

Much of the knowledge and information that goes into a course like a Foundation Degree is embodied within documentation. Roles and responsibilities are laid out in contracts and course structures and outcomes are summarized in handbooks. Standards are formally documented and assessment is normally described in the form of briefs and detailed criteria. In addition to this the resources and materials that support learning and teaching are often also available or at least described in document form, developed jointly by academic provider and employer. This is, after all, the means by which programme providers assert the relevance and quality of their courses and where their roles and responsibilities and those of employers are defined.

Given that opportunities for extended face-to-face collaboration are limited, email can be used for distribution and exchanging materials of this sort. However, this form of communication tends to privilege the sender as it implicitly identifies a producer and one or more consumers of information. An alternative is to provide all stakeholders with access to a repository where they can access and discuss content at various stages of its development (and an example of this has already been discussed in Chapter 4). Some institutions will use systems like Sharepoint or provide their staff with access to software like Adobe Acrobat, which allow documents to be shared and developed collaboratively on the web. However, even if these tools are not available Google Docs and other free-to-use services offer effective alternatives. Even simply allowing an employer access to relevant parts of the VLE can go a long way towards creating an inclusive and dynamic environment for the sharing of information.

Of course, the programme provider will continue to be the author and principle owner of these documents, but the processes by which they are produced, reviewed and maintained can be rendered more transparent and employers can input into these processes in more flexible ways. Email, online forums and other electronic means of communication can then assume a more productive role in facilitating dialogue around the documents and the issues they address. The success of this engagement depends upon many factors. An effective partnership between programme providers and employers requires sophisticated dialogue and close interpersonal relationships and develops over time. However, this transparency can help an education institution to demonstrate good faith and determination in engaging employers in key elements of course design.

Building relationships with the workplace

There are also communication technologies that promote effective dialogue and constructive interpersonal relations. Applications like Skype, Net-meeting and MSN are readily and freely available for people working in educational institutions and allow small groups of individuals to create 'real time' voice or video links between their own respective workplaces (Smith, 2004; Tucker and Neely, 2010). This synchronous form of communication cultivates a personal relationship and facilitates

collaboration and the exchange of information in a more natural con-
versational setting. It allows multiple representatives of employer institutions to be engaged simultaneously, supporting richer and more
inclusive dialogue than is possible in a series of one-to-one or one-
to-many communications. It is also more spontaneous and although
time must be allocated and meetings must be planned in advance, it
is an efficient use of time compared to emails, which require careful
composition, can arrive unexpectedly and take time to read, decode
and respond to. Questions can be asked and responded to immediately and areas of agreement and disagreement can be identified and
dealt with much more emphatically and constructively than in written
communication.

Case study: interactive use of video conferencing

As a senior lecturer on a Foundation Degree for Learning Practitioners I have been
part of a team that has developed e-learning in a number of ways. We actively use
the VLE as a repository for resources including podcasts, course material and web
links. We encourage students to communicate and share experiences on the VLE
and this is particularly important for distance learners. During lectures we develop
the student's use of ICT to support their own and their pupil's learning. We feel
we are open to using ICT creatively for the benefit of our students.

With this in mind when we were teaching students about Every Child Matters(ECM)
we felt it would be beneficial for them to take the theory a step further by talking
with an expert in the field – a Special Educational Needs Co-ordinator (SENCO) in
a large secondary school. Our work was based on the perceived need to make the
boundaries between work in the University College and work in schools (the workplace) less distinct. It was also felt advantageous to access an expert in a field who
would not otherwise have the time to come to college and meet the students and
it also meant that the information received was completely up to date. A dialogue
was possible between the expert and the students which allowed interrogation of
the information in the area.

The practicalities of the situation were that we set up a Skype account on a
computer linked to a whiteboard in the teaching room. The SENCO set up a Skype
account on her laptop. We trialled the video link by connecting with each other and
found this to be quite simple and easy to do. We then arranged a mutually agree-
able time during the teaching session for the video link to take place and called the
SENCO at this agreed time. She spoke briefly about the practicalities involving using

ECM in her school. The students then took it in turns to come up to the microphone and ask her questions about her work.

Evaluations of this whole process by students were extremely positive. Comments included 'It gave insight into how a government policy is introduced and sustained in a large school', 'It was really good to get ready and immediate access to an expert in the field' and overall 'It was a very valuable and memorable experience'. To summarize, students valued the opportunity to access and question an expert in the area. They also highly valued the idea of seeing the impact of what seemed to them very much theoretical concepts directly within a school setting.

Virtual learning environments

Fundamental to any discussion about the role of technology in this area is the concept of the virtual learning environment or VLE. Most education institutions employ dedicated web-based software systems called VLEs, which can be used to deliver documents in a variety of media and to support various forms of web-based communication. They are routinely used to cement links between the programme provider and distance learners and are characterized by the deployment of resources that support progress through formative and marked assignments. In relation to work-based learning they often promote reflection on the relationship between work-based activities and course objectives, promoting communication between dispersed groups of learners and between individual students and their tutors.

However, it is important to move away from a mechanistic focus on a single piece of software, like Moodle or Blackboard. From the student's perspective the virtual learning environment includes all the electronic services provided by the educational institution, including online library services for example, and all the tools and communication technologies that the student can access from the workplace or from home via the internet. The VLE, understood in its broadest form, is therefore not completely within the control or even oversight of the programme provider or the employer. The software packages alluded to above allow institutions to assert a degree of control as hubs or interfaces by providing structure to this environment and mediating student access to it in constructive ways. This creates a significant challenge for programme providers, for developing this kind of resource requires considerable thought and much effort in terms of planning, research and implementation. However, there are opportunities here as well.

For example, the virtual learning environment can be shaped by contributors from different settings. There is no reason why representatives of both education providers and employer institutions cannot participate collaboratively in the learning process, using tools like blogs or discussion forums or technologies like videoconferencing and podcasting. By creating an environment in which representatives of the working and learning environment can come together and interact these two realms, which are held separate in physical space, can be brought together within a virtual environment to support the learner. Seen in this way the online learning environment provides a space where the partnership identified at the beginning of this chapter can develop and differences in terms of values and practices can be addressed in meaningful and constructive ways.

In addition to this there are advantages to be derived from the increasing autonomy and independence that the virtual learning environment confers upon the learner. Foundation Degrees must contribute to the specific professional aspirations of individual learners as well as provide a route to a BA qualification and must therefore accommodate a range of learner expectations and be relevant to the specific practices that exist in the workplace. An effective partnership between programme provider and employer provides an important way of ensuring that this is achieved and a blurring of the boundaries between the worlds of work and learning is empowering for the learner as well. They are better able to see the relevance of their existing skills to their learning and of their learning to their broader professional aspirations. However, it is also important to consider the learner's own place as a member of this partnership, for the Foundation Degree student is primarily located in the workplace and must be relied upon as the principle agent in their learning.

Reflection point

One debate that is regularly applied to courses that contain elements of distance learning concerns the notion transactional distance. Transactional distance is the space that exists between the teacher and the less knowledgeable and less experienced learner. It can be exacerbated by cultural and psychological differences and equates to the potential for teaching to fail or for misunderstandings to arise. However, it is addressed by a range of strategies effecting ways in which the ideas, knowledge and skills encountered within a course are conveyed (structure) and the number, character and quality of the opportunities for communication that occur within the process (dialogue).

Put briefly the concept of transactional distance requires 'teachers' to think about the design of the virtual learning environment: about how the resources are produced and, most importantly, how opportunities for dialogue encourage students to develop and articulate their understanding. In this exercise this dilemma is presented as a series of questions that the reader can apply reflectively to their own provision.

The first questions relate to the structure of the course, or the way in which resources are designed and delivered:

- Do the resources provided cater for the full range of learning issues on the course?
- Have they been designed in ways that cater for a variety of learning styles?
- If students come to the course with different levels of knowledge and experience, do the materials reflect this?
- Have you considered how the design of resources and selection of media impact on motivation?
- Having considered these issues it is then necessary to consider whether students have opportunities for meaningful dialogue around these resources.
- Is communication within the course two way in that students have meaningful opportunities to explore concepts and ideas through dialogue?
- Do students get constructive responses to their contributions to communication?
- Do opportunities for communication require students to analyse the resources they use in critical ways and to apply the values and attitudes associated with the professional environment that they are working in?
- Does dialogue within the course provide students with opportunities to use the skills they are required to develop?
- Do students have opportunities to create knowledge through dialogue and other forms of communication?

The QAA appears to acknowledge this need and recommends that programme providers focus on supporting the development of 'meta-cognitive skills' (Peters, 2005, p. 3) allowing students more control and more ownership over the learning process (QAA, 2010, p. 9). In this sense then we might see technology as providing an environment that affords support and opportunities for students to engage with the fundamental principles and skills that underpin learning, while allowing the employer and the learner themselves to identify the specific working practices around which the actual learning takes place. The learning provider needs to be able to monitor the impact of learning, of course, and given the work-based nature of the course the virtual learning environment can be seen to play a role here as well.

Case study: communication tools on the VLE

The role of the VLE in the Foundation Degree for Learning Practitioners was introduced in the previous case study. It was described as serving as a means of storing and distributing resources in a variety of media and as a means of communication. At one HEI the main areas of VLE development in recent years have involved the use of communication tools and discussion boards in a variety of contexts to facilitate tutor contact, group work and reflective tasks.

However, although the discussion board has many powerful attributes it was felt that it had some limitations too. It is relatively complex to use and it structures information in threads, which can make the content of messages difficult to access. They are, therefore, good for structured tasks or activities that are focused on a specific subject or confined to a specific time frame. However, they are not always the most appropriate platform for an extended discussion that is likely to range across a number of themes and takes place over time.

An example of the latter type of discussion is provided by dialogue around assessment and a blog was chosen as a form of communication tool that might have a useful application here. The blog presents all the content submitted on a single page in the order it was posted and is therefore less sophisticated than the discussion board. However it is easier to monitor, providing one logs in reasonably regularly. What is more it is very easy for people to comment on posts and so the blog suits a situation where people want responses to specific enquiries.

Tutors were able to monitor questions regarding assignments and make interventions where necessary. However, the principle benefit arose from the fact that other students were able to see answers to commonly arising questions, reducing the burden on tutors and were also likely to answer questions directly. Of course misconceptions could arise, but the fact that this discourse was captured in an open forum meant that these could be identified and challenged.

The assessment blog was preferable to email as it reduced the volume of work for tutors and encouraged students to discuss features of the assessment that had caused anxiety in the past. In fact it was very heavily used and referred to on a regular basis by students, who appeared to acquire a sense of ownership of it. This may have been due to the prominence it gave to their questions and the way in which responses could develop and involve a number of people, as questions were clarified and solutions were considered, tested and refined.

This led tutors to consider the value of other online tools that might replace email, which was time consuming and meant that students had to wait for responses. A context was provided by remote tutorials, for Skype, the tool proposed at the out-set, had proven unpopular in this context. Students felt self-conscious in front of a webcam and were daunted by the lack of technical support at home.

Tutors did not want to revert to email so a more synchronous means of communi-cation was sought. Blackboard has chat facilities, known as collaboration tools, but these had proven difficult for some students to use and were unfamiliar in appear-ance. It quickly became clear that students were more comfortable using MSN and so this was explored as an alternative.

MSN proved useful for a number of reasons. First of all it provided an immedi-ate one-on-one encounter with a tutor. However, the fact that students and tutors could see when the other came online meant that tutorials could be conducted flex-ibly, within designated periods of time. Most significantly of all, however, was the fact that the students were largely familiar with this tool and found it very easy to access and very reliable to use from the home PCs. It provided a successful pilot of the principle that the college's VLE could be expanded to encompass tools outside the strict confines of its own software environment.

Learning creatively

Increasingly tools are being introduced into the VLE that attempt to engage with the creative potential of the learner themselves. Features of formal online learning environments like Wikis provide students with enhanced opportunities to create content of their own. They make it easy to create web pages or to upload content from cameras or camcord-ers, or documents produced using software applications that are familiar from the workplace. At the same time sites on the open web that provide opportunities for creative expression, services like Prezi or Glogster, are proliferating and tools like e-portfolios are being used so that students can present their work effectively. Through these means the learner can acquire a higher profile in the virtual learning environment and a more active role in the learning and professional communities in which they are expected to operate. This provides opportunities for assessment by the programme provider, not just on the basis of the learner's creative output, which can be viewed on the VLE, but on their ability to reflect upon the broader relevance of their learning to professional goals as well. This can happen through the use of blogs or discussion forums, perhaps, involving direct communication and interaction with the tutor and with other students.

Using technology to support learning needs

The foregoing discussion has tended to move from a broad treatment of the needs of institutions like programme providers and employers to a more specific focus on the situation and role of students themselves. This increasingly student-centred focus requires us to examine the potential of technology from the perspective of the Foundation Degree student. Many are either new to post-compulsory education or are returning after a break from formal learning and this can mean that technology can be perceived as a barrier, a measure of the extent to which learning environments have moved away from forms familiar to the returning learner. However, computer and internet technologies can be used in a number of ways to support the Foundation Degree student as well.

Services like academic support or learning advice, operations that are normally campus-based and therefore readily available to the full-time resident student are difficult to access by the part-time distance learner. Spaces within the virtual learning environment, properly populated with relevant information and support materials are therefore an important component in any course. In addition to email, discussion boards, blogs and Wikis can provide opportunities for casual, sociable and self-organizing communication with peers and tutors that are, again, commonplace for the conventional learner in higher education, but would otherwise be limited for the Foundation Degree student.

These applications can be seen to provide replacements for services or opportunities that work-based or distance learners find difficult to access, cementing links between the individual learner, the teaching institution and the wider learning community. They are often seen as being benign by institutional management and learners alike as they perform functions that are both comprehensible in terms of traditional patterns of learning and teaching and have a direct impact on the well-being of the learner. They also have a bearing on matters relating to the profile of the institution and issues of financial import like recruitment and retention. In addition such approaches appear unthreatening because they do not intrude into the more fundamental ways in which courses are structured and delivered and do not impact directly on the ways in which students are expected to learn.

Technology and pedagogy

However, many of the applications for technology that we have identified move learning into new realms and require us to question existing practices and to interrogate some of the established values and assumptions associated with higher education. In a certain sense the Foundation Degree provides a good context to rehearse some of these discussions as the Foundation Degree is itself relatively new to the world of higher education. New approaches can be adopted here without appearing to challenge some of the more deeply set and widely held assumptions about course delivery sometimes promulgated by the Academy. However, there is a danger that too close an association will be made between the use of technology and the essentially new conditions imposed by the Foundation Degree. If technology is seen as being nothing more than a solution to the purely practical or logistical problems of work-based learning, then its fullest potential to enhance learning in this context and in wider spheres of higher education will never be realized. In this final section in this chapter we shall attempt to establish the more fundamental links between technology and pedagogy, identifying the role of the tools we have encountered so far within the context of e-learning.

Theorists from all sides of the pedagogical debate have presented visions of e-learning (Jaffer, 2010). In recent years the internet and related technologies have started to move discussion from notions of computer-aided learning, where technology plays a didactic role within the framework of instructional design (Reigeluth, 1999), to a more constructivist approach, which focuses on the ability of technology to engage learners in new patterns of learning through increased social participation (Garner and Gillingham, 1996, p. 16) and more sophisticated forms of critical interaction with information and knowledge (Lankshear et al., 1996). It is important to recognize, therefore, that e-learning is not a separate sphere of pedagogic discussion, but an extension of much wider debates.

In fact we might make explicit links between constructivist pedagogy and the discussion in this chapter. We have looked at the VLE as a place where a community consisting of learners, educators, representatives of employer institutions and members of wider professional networks can form. We have suggested that this aids the learner in a number of ways, principally by helping to create an effective partnership between the employer and the programme provider. However, there is a broader pedagogic issue here as well – one that allows us to consider why this might be desirable for reasons other than the need to overcome logistical challenges – and therefore allows us to look at the contribution of technology in a more nuanced way.

Social constructivism owes many of its founding principles to the work of Piaget (Satterly, 1987), who presented knowledge as a fluid entity that is constructed by the learner according to a largely internal and subjective process of learning, and Vygotsky (1978; Daniels, 2001), who focused on the link between the development of the individual and the wider social context in which they are situated. These ideas have been re-articulated and applied in a number of different ways over the years and a strand of this debate that is relevant to this discussion emerges from Wenger's work on communities of practice (Wenger, 1998). Following Vygotsky's emphasis on the socio-political context in which knowledge is formed, Wenger observes that the processes of learning are only comprehensible within the particular social context in which they are applied. Given this, learning can be seen to be most effective when 'situated' within a broader meaningful context (Lave and Wenger, 1991), one in which students are not only required to work within a community or practice but which requires the student to 'carry out meaningful tasks and solve meaningful problems' (Collins et al., 1989, p. 487). These ideas were also introduced in Chapters 2 and 4.

As we have seen, this approach aligns with the QAA guidance relating to Foundation Degrees, where the focus is placed upon the student's own ownership of the learning process (QAA, 2002, p. 9). We have seen how the virtual learning environment could be used to place this support within a work-based context, where the precise working practices to which those meta-cognitive skills are applied could be defined. Stated baldly the workplace is the space where the learner encounters the community of practice and where the learning outcomes defined by the programme provider are rendered meaningful within a specific professional context. However, the community of practice does not just spring into being and a closer look at Wenger's vision helps to understand both the role of the programme provider and the virtual learning environment from a constructivist perspective.

According to Wenger the community of practice is characterized by domain, community and practice (Wenger et al., 2002). Our approach suggests that the domain, the shared interests or skills that bring the community together, are defined by actors in the workplace, including the individual learner. However, the other two characteristics are yet to be accounted for. The 'community' must be defined by participation in shared activities as well as shared objectives and must actually 'practice' in so far as it allows a clear picture of the practitioner to form, by producing a repertoire of shared tools and experiences. Put another way, for the community of practice to be effective in terms of fostering learning it must act as a community through purposeful activities and must consciously reflect upon these activities and their significance for the individual.

Strictly speaking Wenger's community of practice could and should occur spontaneously whenever people with shared interests or roles gather to further their common purpose. All work-based learners, therefore, might be said to already exist within a community of practice. However, the programme provider and the virtual learning environment can be seen to have an important role to play. This role centres around ensuring that the community of practice encountered in the workplace is able to function in a way that allows the learner to achieve agreed outcomes, by supporting structured activities that all parties can participate in and creating planned opportunities for reflection and consolidation. This might be through the use of specific tools, many of which have been surveyed earlier. However, these outcomes are promoted by the very principle of the virtual learning environment, which creates a flexible environment for collaborative action involving educators, professionals and the learner themselves.

This last point is significant, for in addition to helping to shape the community of practice the learning provider and the virtual learning environment must also help situate the learner so that they can participate in meaningful ways. We have already seen that many features of the virtual learning environment are designed or used in ways calculated to promote the learner's profile through their own active and creative participation in the process and this can be located in the same pedagogic context. For constructivists the belief that knowledge is constructed by the learner requires a shift away from strictly prescribed learning outcomes and the pedagogy that envisages their achievement through preset series of incremental stages. Instead the focus should be on the creative input of the learner in relation to meaningful tasks and problems, both as a means and a measure of learning.

Reflection point

How do your pedagogical beliefs articulate with the notion of technology-enhanced learning?

Conclusion

I have taken a view of the virtual learning environment that accepts the terminology of common parlance in higher education and uses the term VLE to refer to specific, formal web-based learning environments like Moodle and Blackboard. However, I have also used the term more widely to refer to the more global learning environment provided by the World Wide Web. I have suggested that the former is really a form of interface that mediates the learner's engagement with the wider online context in which it is encountered, by providing exemplary resources, links to reviewed content and communication tools that are dedicated to the course.

This acknowledges the essential autonomy of the learner, who will almost certainly see or come to see the World Wide Web as an information space and a place to learn. What is more, where they may be able to passively receive information in the physical learning environment, the online world invites a more active role and requires more developed skills of critical enquiry and evaluation. The internet is not simply a neutral repository, but a place where the user encounters information in a variety of media and from a wide range of sources. It confronts the learner with issues relating to questions of how to learn, forcing them to use discrimination in their use of information and to consider the processes by which knowledge in legitimated within different contexts (Frechette, 2002, pp. 8–9). As such it is a particularly appropriate environment for teaching the meta-cognitive skills that underpin the Foundation Degree course.

The formal part of the virtual learning environment, therefore, supports the student in their engagement with a range of important issues relating to higher learning and provides the context for structured activities in which the learner can both develop and demonstrate their understanding and their progress towards learning objectives. Again this accords with a model that is well suited to the Foundation Degree, but it highlights an important issue that is relevant to the wider context of higher education. Learning technologies, set within the pedagogical framework of the constructivist paradigm, call into question many of the traditional relations between teacher and learner.

The teacher is less privileged in the virtual environment than in the embodied world and the student is necessarily more active and more independent. However, it is not possible to assume that either students or staff are prepared for this situation. Many of the issues that arise from student engagement with the virtual learning environment, inappropriate use of Wikipedia for example, reflect the incomplete state of the learner's transition from an environment where their engagement with resources is prescribed to one in which it is not.

Here the role of the formal virtual learning environment is pivotal, but not because it provides a safe place for learning in the midst of a wider, more dangerous learning environment. Rather it needs to act as a space in which learners consciously work towards perfecting the skills that they need to work effectively within wider professional environments, many of which will have an online dimension and will require engagement with a range of web-based tools and contexts. This further reinforces the importance of the virtual learning environment to the Foundation Degree as it can be seen to situate learning in an environment that is of direct relevance to the wider professional environment for which the student is being prepared. What is more, many of the skills required for learning online can be seen as transferable to the world of work as well.

Summary

This chapter has explored the ways in which e-learning is relevant to Foundation Degrees. By acknowledging the particular role that the workplace takes in the Foundation Degree format, particular consideration has been given to the ways in which learning technologies can support employer engagement and thus enhance the student learning experience. The pedagogical basis for the use of learning technologies has been discussed, in the context of learning as social practice within communities consisting of learners, educators, employers and other stakeholders. Specific consideration has been given to the role of VLEs within Foundation Degree courses.

References

Collins, A., Brown, J. S. and Newman, S. E. (1989), 'Cognitive apprenticeship: teaching the crafts of reading, writing, and mathematics', in Resnick, L. B. (ed.), *Knowing, Learning, and Instruction*. Hillsdale, NJ: Lawrence Erlbaum, pp. 453–494.

Daniels, H. (2001), *Vygotsky and Pedagogy*. New York: Routledge.

Frechette, J. (2002), *Developing Media Literacy in Cyberspace: Pedagogy and Critical Learning for the Twenty-First-Century Classroom*. London: Praeger.

Garner, R. and Gillingham, M. G. (1996), *Internet Communications in Six Classrooms: Conversations Across Time, Space, and Culture*. Mahwah, NJ: Lawrence Erlbaum.

Jaffer, S. (2010), 'Educational technology pedagogy: a looseness of fit between learning theories and pedagogy', *Education as Change*, 14 (2), 273–287.

Lankshear, C., Peters, M. and Knobel, M. (1996), 'Critical pedagogy and cyberspace', in Giroux, H., Lankshear, C., McLaren, P. and Peters, M. (eds), *Counternarratives: Cultural Studies and Critical Pedagogies in Postmodern Spaces*. New York: Routledge, pp. 149–188.

Lave, J. and Wenger, E. (1991), *Situated Learning: Legitimate Peripheral Participation.* Cambridge: Cambridge University Press.

Peters M. D. (2005), 'Foundation Degrees: TheWay Forward for ICT in HE – A Call for Debate on the Design, Implementation and Delivery of ICT Foundation Degrees', *Higher Education Academy*, 4 (2).

QAA (2002), *Foundation Degree Qualification Benchmark.* (2nd edn). Gloucester: QAA.

— (2010), *Foundation Degree Qualification Benchmark.* Gloucester: QAA.

Reigeluth, C. M. (1999), *Instructional-Design Theories and Models: A New Paradigm of Instructional Theory, Volume 2.* Mahwah, NJ: Lawrence Erlbaum.

Satterly, D. (1987), 'Piaget and education', in Gregory, R. L. (ed.), *The Oxford Companion to the Mind.* Oxford: Oxford University Press.

Smith, J. C. (2004), *Effective Use of Desktop Videoconferencing in Teacher Education and Professional Development with Reference to Strategies for Adult Basic Education (Technical Report).* Philadelphia: National Center of Adult Literacy, University of Pennsylvania.

Tucker, J. and Neely, P. (2010), 'Using web conferencing and the Socratic method to facilitate distance learning', *International Journal of Instructional Technology*, 7 (6), 15–23.

Vygotsky, L. S. (1978), *Mind and Society: The Development of Higher Psychological Processes*, Cambridge, MA: Harvard University Press.

Wenger, E. (1998), *Communities of Practice: Learning, Meaning and Identity.* Cambridge: Cambridge University Press.

Wenger, E., McDermott, R. and Snyder, W. M. (2002), *Cultivating Communities of Practice: A Guide to Managing Knowledge.* Boston: Harvard Business School Press.

7 Assessment

Alison Riley

This chapter will:

- provide an overview of what is meant by assessment in higher education
- examine how assessment can be linked to course design
- consider how the work-based experiences of Foundation Degree students can be maximized in the assessment process
- present an overview of the types of assessments which might be utilized in a Foundation Degree
- give guidance as to how students might be prepared for undertaking the assessment process.

What is assessment?

Assessment is generally seen as the most direct 'driver' of study behaviour, not only of the amount of time and effort students put into their work, but also their ways of studying. (Entwistle, 2009, p. 144)

The Quality Assurance Agency (QAA, 2006, p. 6) defines assessment as, 'any process that appraises an individuals' knowledge, understanding, ability or skills'. Assessment can serve a number of purposes and can be of benefit to both the tutor and the student in terms of evaluating the process of learning. For students the assessment process can promote learning through the provision of feedback on assessed work, and will give students a clear indication of their academic performance. For tutors, the assessment process allows them to evaluate the knowledge and understanding of the student body, evaluate their own performance as lecturers and inform future planning.

Assessment is generally described as either summative or formative. Summative assessment evaluates learning at a point in time, whereas formative assessment is designed to provide learners with feedback on progress and inform development. Of course, the distinction between formative and summative assessment is seen by many to be a false one, because whereas some elements of assessment may generate a greater formative learning experience than others, it can be argued that all forms of assessment have some formative element. Indeed, Black and Wiliam (1998), raised the profile of formative assessment in their review of the assessment process in Primary and Secondary Education. This followed over ten years of study into assessment processes, which spanned all educational sectors. Black and William's studies emphasized that assessment should not simply be about passing exams, but should also be an ongoing review of student performance, an approach that is becoming more important for effective learning in higher education (HE) (Sadler, 1989; Crisp, 2007; Nicol and Macfarlane-Dick, undated).

Nicol and Macfarlane-Dick (undated) argue that formative assessment should be an integral part of teaching and learning in higher education, and that both 'feedback' and 'feedforward' should be systematically embedded in curriculum practice. However, Yorke (2003) suggests that whereas formative assessment is acknowledged in HE it may not be widely understood, and in researching the psychology of giving and receiving feedback he notes that this can either be '**constructive** or **inhibitive** towards learning' (2003, p. 477), reiterating the idea that assessment and feedback should be closely linked for students to maximize the potential of the learning experience.

Designing assessment

Chapter 4 has already suggested that a constructively aligned approach to curriculum design is important. By designing the curriculum so that learning activities and assessment tasks are aligned with the learning outcomes that are intended in the course, Biggs (2003, 2005) argues that higher-quality student learning is supported more effectively. For the Foundation Degree student, an extra dimension is added to the notion of constructive alignment as consideration must be given to ways in which learning can be applied to the workplace through the setting of specific tasks which enable students to underpin their practical know-how with reference to appropriate theory.

However, there may well be some disparity between the tutor's view of the assessment process and that of the student. Interestingly, assessment is often the last thing to be planned when writing modules, but frequently the main priority for students when starting a new module. Care must be taken, then, that the curriculum is not driven by what is assessed but rather by what the desired learning outcomes are since an assessment-driven curriculum can potentially result in a surface approach to learning (Marton and Saljo, 1976; Biggs, 1987; Entwistle and Entwistle, 1991; Ramsden, 1992). As already discussed in Chapter 5, in a deep approach students are aiming towards developing a depth of understanding which they might then apply to a wider context, whereas a surface approach to learning is largely about reproducing material to pass a test or examination rather than showing a desire to understand the material which they are being presented with. To some extent Foundation Degree students will adopt a deeper approach to learning since their practical experience of the workplace setting will frequently result in learners who wish to invest time in developing a greater depth of understanding in their chosen field. However, if they are unable to see how the assessment tasks will facilitate this then they may well resort to a more surface approach, simply carrying out tasks to pass the course as opposed to developing their understanding.

Why assess?

Within higher education, assessment should be designed to assure the achievement of standards. The QAA Code of Practice for assessment stipulates that assessment should meet a variety of purposes, including evaluating knowledge, understanding, abilities or skills of students and providing a mark or grade which ensures that student performance can be established. It is the individual student attainment which will provide employers with the confidence that a future employee has 'attained an appropriate level of achievement' (QAA, 2006, p. 4).

The QAA Foundation Degree Benchmark (2010a) recommends that the assessment strategy should reflect the type of learning and learner. Therefore, within the Foundation Degree assessment should be closely linked to workforce development, enabling students to demonstrate the development of knowledge and skills which can be utilized in the workplace. Ideally employers should be involved in the assessment of Foundation Degree programmes, working closely with institutions in the development of assessment practices and in the monitoring of students. The QAA (2010a) recommends, however, that any such arrangements should be agreed from the outset and reviewed regularly to ensure that appropriate standards are maintained. An overriding feature of assessment in Foundation Degrees should of course be in providing for the specific needs of the these students. As stated in the QAA Foundation Degree Benchmark, 'assessment may include a variety of formal and informal, and formative and summative techniques, provided that they are all capable of rigorous testing and independent verification' (2010a, p. 14).

Key principles for Foundation Degree assessment

Appropriate involvement of employers should ensure that assessments are fit for purpose, ensuring that they present the opportunity for students to develop necessary skills within their normal duties. It is important that even if workplace settings do not have a specific role to perform in the assessment process the employer does have an understanding of how the assessment process works, since this ultimately will give employers confidence in the degree course. The QAA Foundation Degree benchmark (QAA, 2010a, p. 6) suggests that there should be a two-way process, 'where the learning in one environment is applied to another', and as such, institution and workplace setting should work closely in maximizing the student learning experience.

Another area of consideration when developing assessments on a Foundation Degree is a need for flexibility, since despite the fact that students studying work in similar settings it is highly likely that their experiences will differ considerably. There is then a danger that some students could be disadvantaged because they do not have access to as wide a range of situations as other students. This is where the involvement of employers can help considerably but it also highlights a need for a more careful approach to developing assessment criteria which might allow for a more flexible approach to assessments. Assessment criteria should be written in such a way that students and tutors can fit the assessment requirement to the specific constraints of a workplace setting, without compromising the need to meet the requirements stipulated by the higher education institution.

Assessment should also be accessible and in this respect the needs of learners with disabilities should be taken into account. The Special Educational Needs and Disability Act (SENDA) introduced in 2001 highlighted the right for students with disabilities not to be discriminated against in education, 'making it unlawful for responsible bodies to treat a disabled person "less favourably" than a non-disabled person for a reason that relates to the person's disability' (SENDA, 2001). Discussion in Chapter 3 has acknowledged that students studying on a Foundation Degree may indeed have distinctive requirements which differ from that of the more traditional undergraduate student, and this coupled with any additional needs that students may have should be borne in mind when planning provision for assessment.

Reflection point

Consider these areas when planning assessment to best meet the needs of all students:

- Do assessment strategies use traditional exam or essay forms – are there better ways of assessing some students with disabilities? Do assessments present a good balance or choice for students?

⇨

- Are adjustments beneficial – can students with disabilities take exams in a peaceful environment or do people taking rest breaks provide a distraction?
- Do submissions by course work carry the same extra time allowance that exams carry or is there a detriment to students undertaking courses assessed mainly through course work?
- Are oral presentations balanced by another option, such as presentations of a DVD for students who are not able to present well orally?
- Are you clear on what you are assessing: the ability to convey information or the information itself?
- Do all essays need to conform to a format or can that information be presented in a variety of formats equally well?

Adapted from Campbell and Norton (2007, p. 135)

The QAA Code of Practice for Students with Disabilities clearly states that 'the assessment methods to be used on programmes should be sufficiently flexible to enable all students to demonstrate that they have met the learning outcomes' (2010b, p. 22), as such adjustments should be made if possible, and alternative assessment methods explored in which students can demonstrate that they have met the intended learning outcome. It is also of utmost importance that feedback given on a piece of work is fully accessible to all students, and it may well be necessary to make reasonable adjustments to the format for presenting feedback to meet the specific needs of all students. This should of course be considered in course design and in monitoring the effectiveness of processes on the programme.

What is being assessed?

Students studying on Foundation Degrees often have a wealth of practical experience, indeed this is often one of the key criteria which must normally be met before the student embarks on the course. One of the dilemmas when writing a Foundation Degree might well be how far assessment should be based around the work they do in their own settings. Although students' roles in their workplace should not be overlooked it is necessary to define whether it is academic ability or workplace capability which is being assessed, since this will ultimately define who is responsible for carrying out assessments. Should work-place capability play a substantial part in the assessment process then it is necessary for professionals within the workplace to take responsibility for carrying out assessments, usually through a mentoring scheme. If this is the case then mentors will need to be trained to meet the Quality Assurance standards of the institution awarding the degree.

A more traditional approach to assessment would be one in which all assessments undertaken by the student are based on academic capabil-ity rather than their professional role, working on the assumption that students are time-served in the workplace and that a certain level of capability can be assumed since employers are willing to support stu-dents in the degree course. Assessing academic capability which takes place solely within the institution provides a certain level of consistency in the assessment process and an assurance that all students are meeting the required standards of the institution, which in turn ensures a level of confidence in the degree as stipulated by the QAA.

However, it is of utmost importance that the student's role in the workplace is fully utilized since 'learning and work are closely inter-linked within Foundation Degree programmes' (QAA, 2010a, p. 6). Assessment provides a perfect opportunity to do this and careful design of assessment activities can allow students to reflect on their prac-tices within the workplace, and through formal assessed work enable them to demonstrate an increased level of theoretical understanding. Consequently, whereas the completion of the assessment process is with the submission of some form of written or oral presentation, the basis of this work is firmly rooted within the practices of the workplace setting.

Who should assess?

Although in this model the responsibility for the formal assessment lies with the institution, the role of the mentor within this should not be overlooked, and a direct link between workplace and educational estab-lishment should be forged wherever possible through the workplace mentor. In many cases students will be expected to carry out tasks in the workplace and a mentor can facilitate this, but perhaps more importantly the workplace mentor can help students to make sense of their observa-tions, having undertaken professional qualifications themselves.

In this way students will begin to recognize that the process of assessment is not just the domain of the university tutor, and although the institution may have responsibility for awarding a final grade, by involving a range of people in the assessment process it is anticipated that students will begin to take greater ownership of their own learning. Nicol and Macfarlane-Dick (undated) make the observation that, 'feedback information is not the sole province of the teacher' and suggest that students should become self-regulating, providing feedback to one another during group activities and generating their own feedback during the academic writing process. Rather than creating dependant students it is desirable that the journey through HE produces interdependent learners, who can draw upon their own skill base to support one another.

Types of assessment

Table 7.1 provides examples of types of assessment 'tried and tested' on a Foundation Degree for Learning Practitioners.

The range of assessments utilized in Table 7.1 presents opportunities for students to demonstrate a range of skills, while maximizing opportunities for workplace experiences to be utilized to their full extent.

Preparing students for assessment

Previous chapters have already explored Foundation Degree learner profiles and have acknowledged that they may be mature age students who have not studied for some time. The process of assessment is a sensitive one, even for the most able student, Light et al. stating that 'it [assessment] can be socially disturbing and divisive for students' (2009, p. 200), suggesting that students may feel that it is not just their learning that is being assessed but their developing identity as people. There is also a school of thought that the assessment process results in a power relationship between tutor and student, with the tutor occupying a dual role of both assisting and passing judgement on the student (Higgins et al., 2002).

As such it is imperative that all students, but particularly those who are non-traditional learners, are introduced to the process of assessment in a way which enables them to achieve early success, since, as the work of

Table 7.1 Assessment types

Example of assessment	Advantages	Disadvantages
Portfolio of tasks *A set of short tasks utilizing a range of skills designed to enable students to demonstrate a breadth of understanding*	Provides opportunities for students to reflect on specific examples from own setting Flexibility of activities allows range of settings to be accommodated Allows for students to reflect upon a range of learning experiences within one module	Skill required in writing to shorter word counts, students need to develop a more analytical approach to writing or work can be overly descriptive Does not always present opportunity to demonstrate a depth of understanding
Essays *A composition on a particular theme or subject*	Presents students with the opportunity to write in greater depth and thereby demonstrate a deeper understanding of the subject matter	Can be subjective in terms of marking, and often time consuming in marking and providing feedback Initially Foundation Degree students can find writing essays a daunting prospect, may require significant guidance in terms of structuring work and writing to the required standard
Case study *A detailed study of an individual unit to find out more about it*	Enables students to examine a particular aspect of practice in their own workplace setting in some detail, opportunity for deep learning to take place. Allows for reflection on an area of professional development, and can enable students to apply theoretical understanding to a particular case	Students can become too involved in a case, and may lose their objectivity, thereby resulting in bias Carefully worded assessment criteria to allow for range of different cases to be accommodated
Examination *A test under timed conditions on a particular theme or aspect*	Allows students to demonstrate personal understanding of a subject matter More time effective for students who are in full-time work	Can lead to surface learning or rote learning whereby students revise information just to pass an exam rather than show any depth of understanding Can lead to excessive anxiety, particularly where students have been out of education for some time Can be time consuming to mark, particularly in the case of longer essay type exams

Assessment type	Pros	Cons
Reports *An account detailing a specific situation or event, usually as a result of an inquiry, written in a specific format*	Presents students with the opportunity to investigate a particular area of choice relevant to own setting or circumstance Set structure for presenting work which supports students in presenting their work Allows students to demonstrate depth of understanding in a particular area	In the first instance students can find it difficult to adapt to the written style of report writing Since students are often given flexibility on the subject matter, based on their own specific experiences, this relies on a wide range of tutor knowledge Assessment criteria must be flexible enough to account for a wide range of topics
Research projects *A work-based longitudinal study into a chosen area using a formal method of enquiry such as Action Research*	Firmly rooted in work-based ethos of degree course, allowing students to demonstrate a depth of understanding pertinent to their own professional needs or the requirements of their work-based setting Students can develop a wide range of skills as a result of conducting formal research.	Can be time consuming in terms of tutor support throughout the duration of the project Students need to ensure that they adhere to the specific requirements of carrying out academic research e.g. reliability, validity, ethics.
Presentations (group, paired, individual) *An oral or visual means by which to demonstrate knowledge and understanding of a particular area or theme*	Opportunity for students to demonstrate different skill sets to that of more formal academic writing Enables tutor to gauge level of understanding of individual students	Group presentations rely on good communication between students, a group can be put at a disadvantage if not all participants are co-operative Can be subjective in terms of assessing individuals Can lead to high levels of anxiety for some individuals
Discussions /debates *Verbal presentation of ideas and opinions designed to assess a depth of knowledge*	Enables students to demonstrate a depth of understanding, particularly when responding to others in the group	Needs some degree of moderation, particularly where there are dominant members of a group Can be difficult to assess
Multimedia *Utilizes technology including wikis, blogs and presentation software*	Enables students to demonstrate a range of IT skills Motivating as a different form to the more traditional assessment types	Can be challenging to students who do not have technology skills Open to IT 'gremlins'

Smith (2007) reveals, a mismatch between student expectations and abilities can result in high dropout rates. Students who are keen to develop their professional skills may well have gained Level 3 qualifications prior to embarking on a Foundation Degree course, and often assume that success in these may be easily transferable to the Level 4 course.

The work of Lea and Street (1998) perhaps goes some way in providing an explanation for this since they recognize that academic writing is one of the main difficulties which students encounter as they enter HE, and while Level 3 qualifications demand that students demonstrate practical skills, and evidence these through written accounts, at Levels 4 and 5, students are being asked to reflect in more depth on their experiences, and relate these to theoretical underpinnings. It is 'trying to unpack the ground rules of writing in any particular context' (Lea, 2004, p. 740) which presents the most challenge for these students. Although it could be argued that not all assessments require a written element, the vast majority do and as such to maximize the potential for success, first and foremost students must be taught how to present work for academic purposes. Returning to the work of Lea and Street, this process of presenting work for academic purposes they would refer to as 'study skills', and includes the basic structures of written work, correct referencing and the use of correct English. In addition students must also demonstrate an ability to reflect on their workplace role, analysing and evaluating this through their writing and relating it to their understanding of educational theory; Lea and Street refer to these stages as 'academic socialisation' and 'academic literacies'. Lea and Street do not see these stages as linear but as integral to the writing process. It is, then, a challenge for the tutor to ensure that appropriate support is given, so that students are fully prepared for all aspects of the assessment process. These issues are discussed fully in Chapter 3, but in general it is fair to say that a structured approach is desirable, and may be achieved through taught sessions, study skills sessions and tutorials. Ideally this should be progressive, enabling students to build upon and develop skills through the duration of the course, with support gradually being reduced as students become more confident in their academic ability.

From a purely practical point of view, students should have clear assignment briefs that outline the required assessment and criteria for achievement. A sample assignment brief can be found in Appendix 6.

Feedback and feedforward

The QAA states that, 'institutions should ensure that appropriate feedback is provided to students on assessed work in a way that promotes learning and facilitates improvement' (QAA, 2006, p. 10) and students who invest time in their work will expect a similar investment from their tutors by way of detailed feedback. This can be pivotal to the esteem of the student studying on the Foundation Degree.

Tutors' response to students' work should perform three specific functions:

1. Marking or grading: providing a mark or a grade gives students a measure of their performance against assessment criteria. For the institution, the marking process can provide a level of confidence in the academic standard achieved by the student.
2. Feedback: provides a commentary on areas of strength and weakness on a specific assessment task and should be termed in such a way that encourages and motivates the student.
3. Feedforward: has the potential to be the most important part of the process since if worded carefully students should be able to apply the comments in the feedforward in a developmental way, enabling them to improve areas of their academic work.

However, providing feedback is not without its problems (Higgins et al. 2001; Crisp, 2007; Race, undated) and if it is to serve the purpose of enabling students to develop then the process should be considered carefully.

Perhaps one of the most significant areas of dissatisfaction for both students and tutors is the timeliness of the feedback. As most programmes are governed by institutional requirements, it is frequently the case that by the time students have received feedback the specific module on which the feedback is based is complete, and it is too late to address any issues which might arise. This can be alleviated by providing a clear distinction between feedback and feedforward, with the feedforward creating a generic link between observations from one assessment, and suggesting targets for improvement which can be applicable to a range of assessments rather than being specific to one type.

Race (undated) recommends that feedback should be given to students as soon as possible after the assessment, ideally within a day or two. He suggests that this will maximize the effectiveness of the feedback since the work is still fresh in the mind of the students, and although it could be suggested that this is still too late for it to impact on the work which students have just completed it may well be effective in preparing students as they begin their next assessment.

Race also states that, 'feedback should open doors not close them' (undated), and warns that tutors should take care in the wording used when giving feedback. An overly negative use of language may have serious implications for the relationship between tutors and students, whereas a wholly positive response may well demotivate students, since it will require the student to maintain a level from one assignment to the next. This may not be possible given the range of assessment types frequently used on programmes; for instance, a student who writes a good essay may not be as adept when to comes to report writing. To minimize the effects of this, Race suggests the approach should be to praise specific aspects of work in more detail rather than limiting the feedback to generic adjectives.

Another area which should not be overlooked when providing feedback to students is that of the language and terminology used, since feedback can only be of value if the students understand what is being asked of them, and more importantly can translate that into a meaning which will enable them to build on and develop their academic skills. It is important that we are mindful of the specific nature of the Foundation Degree student in this instance, since as has already been acknowledged they may well have been absent from formal education for some time, and it cannot be assumed that they will automatically be able to interpret the comments they have been given. If only vague, single sentence comments are provided as a means of feedforward then it should also be the case that some sort of further support is offered to students by way of tutorials or study skills sessions, particularly as students first embrace learning in Higher Education. It is the role of the tutor not just to provide feedback, but also to monitor its effectiveness, providing appropriate support as required.

Learner voice

Sometimes feedback is useful but it would be better if we were told how to rectify problems, the issues could be highlighted within the work, rather than just referred to in general on the feedback sheet. I am never sure if an issue is with the whole of my work or just parts of it.

⇨

> Feedback could be developed by pointing out which parts are good, and guidelines as to why it was good and more depth. Equally, I know we are given targets, but ideas as to how it could be improved in the feedback, which I know has to be positive, but something like 'Such and such an area is good but if you did this. . . . it would enhance it'.
>
> I find targets really useful as I try and give 110 per cent on all my assignments, so if it was something I already knew I should be doing, I would hopefully be doing it. These give me something else to aim for.

It is important then, that students are supported in engaging with their feedback. Appendix 7 contains an example resource that has been used with Foundation Degree students to do this.

Conclusion

If planned with care the assessment process on a Foundation Degree can fulfil a number of important roles. Essentially the process will provide a measure of how well a student is doing on the programme, and also enable tutors on the course to consider how far the teaching on the course meets the intended requirements of the programme, and ultimately the institution awarding the degree. This in turn provides employers with the confidence that graduates from the institution have met the necessary standards to take on increasingly responsible roles in the workplace, or as may well be the case with the Foundation Degree student it provides them with a qualification to enable them to continue their education to honours degree level, thereby opening up more opportunities in the professional workplace.

Maximizing the potential of the assessment process is a challenge. However, careful planning can present opportunities for the process to not only be used as a means for measuring student capability, but perhaps more importantly encourage students to reflect on their everyday experiences, and learn from them, creating a holistic learning experience for the students. This in turn meets the agenda for the Foundation Degree of professionalizing the workforce.

Summary

To ensure that both students and tutors reap the benefits of the assessment process consideration must be given to each stage, from planning a wide range of assessment experiences which will enable students to take full advantage of opportunities in both the workplace and the educational establishment. Appropriate and timely support should be given so that students have the best chance of success, and finally feedback given to the students should be such that it allows students to develop as learners.

References

Biggs, J. B. (1987), *Student Approaches to Learning and Studying*. Melbourne: Australian Council for Educational Research.

Biggs, J. (2003), *Teaching for Quality Learning at University*. Buckingham, UK: SRHE/Open University Press.

— (2005), *Aligning Teaching for Constructive Learning*. Higher Education Academy. Available online at: www.heacademy.ac.uk/assets/York/documents/resources/resourcedatabase/id477_aligning_teaching_for_constructing_learning.pdf (accessed 23 January 2011).

Black, P. and Wiliam, D. (1998), *Inside the Black Box: Raising Standards through Classroom Assessment*. London: Kings College.

Campbell, A. and Norton, L. (2007), *Learning, Teaching and Assessing in Higher Education*. Exeter: Learning Matters.

Crisp, B. (2007), 'Is it worth the effort? How feedback influences students subsequent submissions of assessed work', *Assessment and Evaluation in Higher Education*, 32 (5), 571–581.

Entwistle, N. (2009), *Teaching for Understanding at University*. London: Palgrave Macmillan.

Entwistle, N. J. and Entwistle, A. C. (1991), 'Contrasting forms of understanding for degree examinations: the student experience and its implications', *Higher Education*, 22, 205–227.

Higgins, R. Hartley, P. and Skelton, A. (2001), 'Getting the message across: the problem of communicating feedback', *Teaching in Higher Education*, 6 (20), 269–274.

— (2002), 'The conscientious consumer: reconsidering the role of assessment feedback in student learning', *Studies in Higher Education*, 27, 1.

Lea, M. R. (2004), 'Academic literacies: a pedagogy for course design', *Studies in Higher Education*, 29 (6), 739–758.

Lea, M. R. and Street, B. V. (1998), 'Student writing in higher education: an academic literacies approach', *Studies in Higher Education*, 23 (2), 157–171.

Light, G., Cox, R. and Calkins, S. (2009), *Learning and Teaching in Higher Education: The Reflective Professional*. London: Sage.

Marton, F. and Saljo, R. (1976), 'On qualitative differences in learning – I: outcome and process', *British Journal of Educational Psychology*, 46, 4–11.

Nicol, D. and Macfarlene-Dick (undated), *Rethinking Formative Assessment in HE: A Theoretical Model and Seven Principles of Good Feedback Practice*. Available online at: www.heacademy.ac.uk/assets/York/documents/ourwork/assessment/web0015_rethinking_formative_assessment_in_he.pdf (accessed 22 February 2011).

QAA (2006), *Code of Practice for the Assurance of Academic Quality and Standards in Higher Education; Section 6 Assessment of Students*. Available online at: www.qaa.ac.uk/Publications/InformationAndGuidance/Pages/Code-of-practice-Section-6.aspx (accessed 23 January 2011).

— (2010a), *Foundation Degree Qualification Benchmark*. Gloucester: QAA.

— (2010b), *Code of Practice for the Assurance of Academic Quality and Standards in Higher Education; Section 3 Disabled Students*. Available online at: www.qaa.ac.uk/Publications/InformationAndGuidance/Pages/Code-of-practice-Section-3.aspx (accessed 22 February 2011).

Race, P. (undated), *Using Feedback to Help Students Learn*. Higher Education Academy. Available online at: http://phil-race.co.uk/wp-content/uploads/Using_feedback.pdf (accessed 13 April 2011).

Ramsden, P. (1992), *Learning to Teach in Higher Education*. London: Routledge.

Sadler, D. R. (1989), 'Formative assessment and the design of instructional systems', *Instructional Science*, 18, 119–144.

Smith, R. (2007), 'An overview of research on student support: helping students to achieve or achieving institutional targets? Nuture or de-nature', *Teaching in Higher Education*, 12 (5), 683–695.

Special Educational Needs and Disability Act (SENDA) (2001). Available online at: legislation.gov.uk (accessed 23 January 2011).

Yorke, M. (2003), 'Formative assessment in higher education: moves towards theory and the enhancement of pedagogic practice', *Higher Education*, 45, 477–501.

Looking to the Future

Claire Taylor

This chapter will:

- look holistically at issues raised in earlier chapters
- suggest ways to 'future-proof' the Foundation Degree student experience through a consideration of learning enablers and inhibitors
- consider the future for Foundation Degrees in the context of political changes to the further and higher education landscape.

Bringing key ideas together

Each chapter in this book has considered a particular aspect of Foundation Degree learning and teaching and it is hoped that readers have felt able to 'dip in' to particular chapters as they seem pertinent to their practice. However, it is worth pausing and considering the themes that have recurred throughout this book to form a more rounded view of the Foundation Degree student experience.

In Chapter 1, I outlined that the Foundation Degree represents a distinctive higher-level, work-based, vocational qualification. The distinctiveness is dependent upon not only its work-based nature, but also upon the integration of certain characteristics – namely employer involvement, accessibility, articulation and progression, flexibility and partnership (QAA, 2010). The characteristics have been explored within the different contexts of each of the chapters within this book and have therefore been viewed through a number of lenses: learner needs, course design, learning and teaching approaches, e-learning and assessment. Within each of these areas there are strands related to the learner, tutor and workplace and it is important to consider these strands both individually and relationally to gain a holistic picture of learning and teaching within a Foundation Degree.

Future-proofing your Foundation Degree

Student learning does not happen in isolation and therefore it is important to consider the individual and relational roles of learners, employers and tutors within Foundation Degrees to 'future-proof' Foundation Degree learning and teaching and assure a first-rate student experience. Previous chapters have highlighted a number of factors that impact

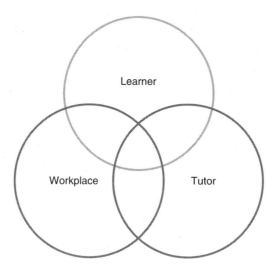

Figure 8.1 Learning and teaching on Foundation Degrees – a relational Venn diagram

upon the learner experience – factors linked to the learner themselves, the workplace and the tutors. However, these factors are also interrelated and the interactions between learner, tutor and workplace can be usefully depicted as a Venn diagram (Figure 8.1). By showing the possible relational combinations of learner, tutor and workplace in this way, a more rounded view of the Foundation Degree experience may be appreciated.

I would suggest that the quality of the Foundation Degree student experience depends not only upon the individual roles of learner, tutor and workplace, but also upon the nature of these relational interactions. This leads to a range of possible factors and relational combinations that could influence learning and teaching:

- the learner
- the tutor
- the workplace
- the learner-tutor interface
- the learner-workplace interface
- the workplace-tutor interface
- the learner-tutor-workplace interface.

Furthermore, Figure 8.2 shows that any one of these factors or relational combinations could be situated along a continuum that inhibits or enables learning. Therefore, it is important that the Foundation Degree tutor has a good understanding of the possibilities that are presented for learning inhibition or enablement within the contexts of course design, delivery and assessment.

The following section draws upon empirical research conducted with Foundation Degree students over a two-year longitudinal period (Taylor, 2009). The study sought to understand and articulate those factors that may inhibit or enable Foundation Degree learning through a case study approach of one small group's experiences of learning. In addition the

Figure 8.2 The learning inhibitors/enablers continuum

study made practical suggestions for developing strategies to mitigate the effects of learning inhibitors and enhance the positive impact of potential learning enablers. The following factors are considered here:

- the learner: self-theories, resilience and motivation
- the tutor: beliefs, attitudes and roles
- the workplace: employer engagement and work-based learning opportunities.

Reflection point

The factors outlined in the following section are those that emerged from one specific study with a small group of Foundation Degree learners. Different factors may emerge with a different group of Foundation Degree learners and/or tutors.

How could you use the Venn diagram framework (Figure 8.1) as a tool for exploring what influences Foundation Degree learning and teaching in your setting?

The learner: self-theories, resilience and motivation

Many students have expectations of higher education study shaped not only by their views of self (Dweck, 2000; Reay, 2003) but also by a range of personal dispositions (Barnett, 2007) and motivational factors (Maslow, 1970).

Dweck's (2000) work around self-theories underlines the advantage that a student has if their self-belief is founded upon a malleable form of ability – a 'can do' attitude that perseveres in terms of seeking self-improvement. Self-theories are the belief systems that learners have regarding the mutability of an attribute such as intelligence. Dweck distinguishes between entity and incremental beliefs – or fixed versus malleable views of intelligence:

> Some people believe that their intelligence is a fixed trait. They have a certain amount of it and that's that. We call this an 'entity theory' of intelligence because intelligence is portrayed as an entity that dwells within us and that we can't change. Other people have a very different definition of intelligence. For them intelligence is not a fixed trait that they simply

possess, but something they can cultivate through learning. We call this an 'incremental theory' of intelligence because intelligence is portrayed as something that can be increased through one's efforts. (Dweck, 2000, pp. 2–3)

Dweck's premise is that the student who believes the 'entity theory' of intelligence can become worried about how intelligent they are. This results in them striving to appear intelligent, and therefore less likely to take risks in their learning as they do not want to make mistakes. In contrast, self-esteem in the incremental system becomes something that learners can achieve for themselves through making an effort with their learning, and this view motivates students to learn.

For the Foundation Degree student, whether they adopt an entity or incremental self-theory could have an impact upon their learning experience as well as sense of self. In their work considering the implications of self-theories for teaching and learning in higher education, Yorke and Knight (2004) contend that:

> Students with entity beliefs tend to adopt performance goals, that is, they seek to demonstrate and confirm their (believed fixed) level of ability, and to avoid outcomes that would undermine this. Incremental self-theorists, on the other hand, tend to adopt learning goals, seeing the challenges they face as being opportunities for learning. (Yorke and Knight, 2004, p. 27)

In this respect, in the context of self-belief being framed by an incremental view of learning, the personal element to learning effectively comes to the fore and becomes an important factor in achieving success.

Case study: Kat

For Kat, even applying to university was a huge step to take and the research revealed that Kat in particular struggled with the development of an academic identity and continually doubted her ability to succeed throughout the course. Kat's social and cultural background had engendered a particular view of the type of person who may succeed at university. She really believed that 'only clever people get degrees [. . .] people who are in high powered jobs'. Kat doubted her ability to succeed, and suggested that there was a limit to what she could achieve as, by implication, she did not view herself as 'clever'. Kat was exhibiting learned helplessness (Dweck, 2000), and such a perception of herself was in danger of inhibiting her learning. Kat had a poor view of her ability to succeed and therefore low aspirations in terms of studying within higher education.

Also vital to success is resilience on the part of the student. Barnett suggests that students generally operate in a state of anxiety, operating within the context of a higher education which contains a 'pedagogy of challenge' and therefore which 'calls for qualities of resilience and fortitude' (Barnett, 2007, p. 54). Barnett contends that ' "Will" is the most important concept in education' (Barnett, 2007, p. 15). Indeed without a will to learn, the student cannot move forward into new learning situations; it is the will that contributes to students completing their course of higher education study. Encouragingly, evidence suggests that Foundation Degree learners do possess this 'will' as 80 per cent of those who started Foundation Degree courses in 2002 gained the Foundation Degree qualification or higher (HEFCE, 2007); yet, the positioning of a Foundation Degree learner upon a continuum related to resilience may affect their studies.

Barnett, however, makes a clear distinction between 'will' and 'motivation', describing a motive as 'essentially rational' (Barnett, 2007, p. 16) – in other words, a reason for doing something towards an end. In contrast, 'will', Barnett argues, is non-rational and is independent of reason. Will is more general and internal to the person concerned, whereas motivation is more specific in character and is in the form of an object or interest external to a person. Yet, motivating factors can be as basic as meeting physiological needs (food, water, shelter) or as profound as self-actualization – 'a person's desire to become all that he or she is capable of becoming' (Merriam et al., 2007, p. 282). Such factors were incorporated by Maslow (1970) into a progressive order of human needs, or hierarchy, starting with physiological needs and moving through safety, social esteem and self-actualization needs. In the study I have outlined, the Foundation Degree students were motivated by a need to improve employment prospects, suggesting a motivating factor fairly low down on Maslow's hierarchy.

> **Reflection point**
>
> Do you know what motivated your students to engage in Foundation Degree study? Does this have implications for how you design and deliver your Foundation Degree?

Therefore, for the Foundation Degree student, factors such as self-theory, resilience and motivation may significantly impact upon their learning experience, depending upon the extent to which they are acting as learning enablers or inhibitors. This may be true even at pre-application stage and so (as already discussed in Chapter 3) involvement with aspiration-raising activities during pre-application could be critical in establishing a positive decision to apply. In addition a 'taste' of higher education study, in the form of 'taster days' or residential summer schools could allay fears and serve as a stepping stone towards applying for higher-level study – again these have been outlined in Chapter 3. Activities such as these have the potential to raise aspirations among prospective Foundation Degree course applicants, enabling them to begin the student life cycle with an optimistic self-view in relation to academic capability and a more intrinsically embedded motivational framework, thus moving them along the continuum from learned helplessness to learned optimism.

The tutor: beliefs, attitudes and roles

In acknowledging that students' self-theories may impact upon achievement, there is, by implication, a further factor related to tutor beliefs regarding ability. Regarding self-theories in particular, Yorke and Knight (2004) identify key implications for the tutor role in relation to the beliefs they hold. For example, where a tutor is situated along the 'fixed to malleable' continuum may dictate the nature and level of support they may offer to a student and therefore tutors' self-theories could have a significant effect upon the cultivation of positive student self-theories and upon student attainment. A tutor situated towards the fixed end of the fixed–malleable continuum would be in danger of imposing a severe inhibitor upon student achievement – particularly if they reinforced a student's self-theory that tended towards a fixed view. For a tutor aware of self-theories, then, the challenge would have been to support a student such as Kat (see case study) in moving towards a more malleable view of ability. What would not have been helpful to a student such as Kat would have been contact with a tutor who held fixed views on ability. For any learner, and perhaps for 'non-traditional' Foundation Degree students in particular, being labelled as working 'at the right level for their ability' (with the implication that potential achievement was capped at a certain level) could potentially act as a learning inhibitor.

Chapter 3 made the case that many Foundation Degree learners were uncertain about what to expect of higher education and whether they were capable of succeeding within the unfamiliar environment of 'the academy'. Such uncertainties could be linked to self-theories regarding ability, already discussed earlier, but could also be connected to a lack of understanding of higher education systems and expectations. Therefore, the teaching team has a crucial role in supporting student access to the academy. For example, Chapter 3 has already explored the need for support pre-course in terms of raising aspirations, and in terms of demystifying elements of academic practice to improve accessibility to higher education for non-traditional students. Such support needs to continue throughout induction and into semester one and beyond, to mitigate the barriers to participation in higher education identified by Gorard et al. (2006) and to dispel the anxieties felt by Foundation Degree students from non-traditional backgrounds in particular (Bowl, 2003; Reay, 2003). This would then have the potential of enabling access to the academy.

When working with work-based learners, the emphasis for the role of the tutor moves away from the transmission of knowledge, to supporting the learners in incorporating information into their own frame of reference (Mezirow, 1997) and facilitating the interactive exploration of the ideas and knowledge that students may bring with them (Hockings et al., 2007). In addition, in responding to the non-traditional student, tutors may have to take account of the students' lack of prior engagement with academic practices and unfamiliarity with academic language. In this respect, tutors find traditional, didactic teaching practices ineffective (Street, 1984) and need, instead, to value and draw upon what the students know.

Such a role demands of the tutor not only knowledge of the workplace in question and the practices that are carried out within the workplace, but also an appreciation of the multidimensional quality of workplace learning (Billett, 2002) and a scholarly knowledge and understanding of theory relevant to the particular area of learning being undertaken. This is so that students can be supported in moving beyond the immediate context and show awareness of their learning in a new situation (Boud, 2001), a skill associated with study at the higher education level (QAA, 2008). Fundamentally, though, the tutor must appreciate the nature of work-based learning and embrace the acceptance of different forms of knowledge and the credible contribution that they can make to a student's learning, as discussed previously in Chapter 2.

Therefore, it is helpful to view the tutor as facilitator, rather than as a transmitter of knowledge. Gregory (2002) defines facilitation as a role that seeks to draw out from the learner already existing wisdom. This role also depends upon the tutor holding a view of knowledge that recognizes the worth of different types of knowledge and the importance of helping the learner to move beyond the immediate context to transform and reinvent knowledge in different contexts (Fenwick, 2000; Boud, 2001). In addition, the tutor is charged with recognizing the links between experience and abstract ideas within the learning process (Kolb, 1984) and in supporting the student in developing a reflective approach to make sense of such links (Moon, 1999). Therefore, where the tutor's role is placed along the continuum between acting as knowledge transmitter and learning facilitator could inhibit or enable the students' learning. It should be clear, though, that the tutor's role is a complex one. For example, in relation to the place of reflection in learning, Moon refers to the process as a 'messy' one 'with stages re-cycling and interweaving as meaning is created and recreated' (Moon, 1999, p. 35). The tutor has to help the student make sense of this in the context of what the student brings to their learning – including their identity and the 'complexities of human experience' (Fenwick, 2000, p. 244).

Earlier in this chapter, I discussed the need for a student to have a 'will to learn' and the tutor has a role in nurturing it. For Barnett, nurturing the student's 'will to learn' not only necessitates commitment by the tutor, over a sustained period of time, to support the student's learning journey, it also involves the tutor giving the student 'space' to learn so that 'students can become authentically themselves' (Barnett, 2007, p. 141). Furthermore, Barnett describes a 'spatial tension' between the 'singularity' of permitting a student 'to become what she wishes' and the 'universiality' of knowing that the student will be judged by specific standards within the field. Similarly, Yorke and Knight (2004, p. 34) highlight the marginalization of the 'personal dimension of student learning' because of the growing emphasis in higher education upon the attainment of measurable task outcomes and standards. Therefore, the tutor also has a role in managing the tensions inherent in nurturing a student's learning journey through enabling pedagogical spaces, and retaining an awareness of the standards embedded in the course of study. In this respect the Foundation Degree format is well placed to cope with such a tension. For example, the work-based elements have the potential to be tailored to the interests of the student, and in this way pedagogical space can be created in which the student can engage in their own explorations, reflecting upon both workplace and higher education studies, and seeing connections between the two.

Case study: pedagogical space

Max, a first year student, describes how the Foundation Degree course gives 'space' within which to reflect and make connections between the workplace and the course content:

> As time goes on and through experience and through being reflective you see those connections and make those connections more and more . . . The lights go on, because then when you go back into your workplace the next day you think oh I know why that's happening or you know suddenly you can see the relevance of things.

Therefore, for Max, the combination of their work-based experience and higher education studies provided a meaningful overall learning experience, rooted in both workplace practice and academic rigour.

The workplace: employer engagement and learning opportunities

Employer engagement with Foundation Degrees at all stages of design and delivery has been a recurring theme throughout this book (see

Chapters 3 and 4 in particular) but commentators suggest that engaging employers in the design and delivery of Foundation Degrees has been less than successful (Foskett, 2003; Brennan and Gosling, 2004; Duckworth, 2006; Green, 2006). Indeed, if we were to situate employer engagement along a continuum from acting as learning inhibitor to learning enabler, we may find in the majority of cases that it is situated towards the 'disinterested' node rather than the 'active partnership' node. This is despite the fact that Foundation Degree courses should be cognizant of the QAA (2010) benchmark that states explicitly that employers will be involved in the design and review of courses and, ideally, in course delivery, assessment and the monitoring of students. In addition, regardless of the requirements of the QAA it makes good sense to involve employers in the Foundation Degree to ensure relevance in relation to the work-based elements.

It seems essential, then, that employers are engaged more fully before a student even applies for a Foundation Degree, at the very beginning of the student life cycle. Indeed Hulbert (2007) argues that employer engagement 'does need to be better understood and articulated as a longitudinal continuum of partnership' (Hulbert, 2007, p. 13), and perhaps the continuum needs to span from before a student makes an application for a Foundation Degree course, in the hope that engagement would then continue throughout the course. This would demand more effort on the part of the higher education institution, at least initially, to market the Foundation Degree to potential work-based partners. Leitch (2006) advocates that higher education providers should be more responsive to what learners and employers want, and is also clear that the Foundation Degree provides one resource that should be promoted to fill the gap in adult skills. Yet there still appears to be misunderstanding from some employers as to what the Foundation Degree actually is and even suspicion in some sectors as to whether the qualification will actually meet the needs of the learner and the employer (Brennan, 2004; Green, 2006). Perhaps one way forward would be for employers to be more actively involved in partnership with the student from earlier on in the process – for example, by attending course open days together, and even having a joint input at the interview stage. This may go some way in moving the nature and level of employer engagement from disinterest to active partnership and would provide a platform for the employer's ongoing involvement in supporting the learner's experience in the workplace (discussed further later in this chapter).

I would suggest that the higher education institution should take the lead in engaging more proactively with employers, to foster an active partnership with employers and the best possible work-based learning experience for students. This may include the development of a general programme of support for employers, with roles and responsibilities clearly outlined; the use of specific staff to liaise with the workplace, and specific training related to the mentoring role in particular (mentoring is discussed in the next paragraph). Such initiatives may be able to pre-empt the difficulties of engaging with employers once the course has started. In addition, the use of contracts (discussed in Chapter 4), drawn up between the higher education institution, the employer and the student may serve to formalize the partnership arrangement more clearly in terms of setting out roles and responsibilities for all parties.

Mentoring is briefly suggested by the Foundation Degree benchmark (QAA, 2010) as one vehicle for supporting students in the workplace, but is not promoted within government rhetoric as an essential manifestation of either employer involvement or a commitment to ensuring a quality experience for the learner in the workplace. However, Herde and Rohr paint an ideal picture of how mentoring within the workplace could be beneficial to all parties involved in Foundation Degree delivery:

> Mentoring not only benefits the mentee (the student) but also the mentor and the company as a whole. The benefits are higher levels of competence, closer working relationships with the teaching institution, across section and departments and between different levels of the organisation, increased motivation and overall improved outcomes. In this way effective mentoring can raise achievement, self-confidence, personal and social skills for all involved. (Herde and Rohr, 2005, p. 15)

This picture of mentoring practice goes beyond merely being a structure to demonstrate employer engagement. Instead, it aspires to transform workplace experience and performance as well as foster more effective relationships with the higher education institution, leading to extended participation for the work-based learner. Yet, the key area identified as an aspect where there seemed to be extremes in terms of successful practice for the case study students was the practice of mentoring in the workplace.

Case study: contrasting support in the workplace

Jill was studying for an education-related Foundation Degree and described very positive attitudes from teaching colleagues at school towards her studies including the work-based elements. At the end of the first year, she stated: 'All the teachers at our school have been so supportive.' The nature of support seemed to be practical and responsive to Jill's needs in relation to the course, and to work-based tasks in particular: 'The Year 6 teacher I worked with last year she's always trying to find out how I'm getting on. I'll nip up to see her [and ask] can I borrow children for an interview and things like that.' There appeared to be a willingness from all staff to take an interest in what Jill was doing and this was aided further by the experience of Jill's workplace mentor. The mentor had already seen a student through the same Foundation Degree (that student is now a qualified teacher in the school) and clearly understood what the course entailed, particularly in relation to the work-based tasks. Jill explained, 'She has actually said a couple of times "I've got a great task coming up if you need anything to do," because she knows.' 'Knowing' was the key thing for Jill here and my interpretation of this went beyond the mentor's knowledge of the course as described in the course handbook, but further to embrace some knowledge of what it meant to engage in the course – of what it really meant to learn through a Foundation Degree.

In contrast to Jill, Guy experienced very different levels of support within the workplace. It appeared limited or even non-existent compared to fellow Foundation Degree students: 'When you talk to other people you think "mmm, you know they're getting quite a lot of support aren't they."' Workplace colleagues seemed to have very little understanding of what Guy was engaged in: 'I don't think actually the other staff realize what it is I'm doing either.' More effective mentoring practice could have improved the work-based learning experience for Guy, moving him along the continuum from restricted participation to extended participation.

Therefore, it could be suggested that higher education institutions have an obligation to ensure that clear policies are in place for ensuring that effective workplace learning takes place. In terms of workplace mentoring, Darwin (2000) outlines different views on what constitutes high quality mentoring, including the functionalist perspective (where knowledge is transferred from mentor to mentee), and the perspective which has at its core the notion of a more interdependent mentor-mentee relationship, which encourages co-learning and dialogue. For Foundation Degree learners, the functionalist role is a vital one – particularly in enabling them to undertake work-based tasks set by the HEI. Such a role is also important in terms of ensuring that information is passed on swiftly between higher education institution, student and workplace – particularly as Green found that the exchange of information seemed to be a cause for concern with some partnerships, suggesting that course staff 'need to be sure to target the right person' (Green, 2006, p. 30).

Reflection point

What mechanisms do you have in place for engaging employers in the design and delivery of your Foundation Degree? Refer to Chapter 4 for information around workplace agreements and developing employer partnerships.

To what extent do the quality of workplace learning opportunities enable or inhibit learning for your students?

The future for Foundation Degrees

Foundation Degrees have become an established part of the further and higher education landscape in England and Wales. The years 2009–2010 saw the ninth consecutive year-on-year growth for student enrolments on Foundation Degrees (HEFCE, 2010) and government rhetoric from both current and previous administrations, and their advisors, continues to emphasize the need for both skills development among the UK population and continued widening of access to higher education. For example, in 2009 the government's 'Higher Ambitions' report made some clear statements regarding the potential for further growth in flexible provision (including in Foundation Degrees) to support the government's skills strategy:

> In order to attract a greater diversity of students, more part-time study, more vocationally-based foundation degrees, more work-based study and

more study while living at home must be made available. This is a core aim of these proposals, and our wider skills strategy. (BIS, 2009, p. 3)

Following 'Higher Ambitions', Lord Browne was charged with reviewing the funding of higher education and making recommendations to ensure that higher education teaching was sustainably financed and of world class quality, and that higher education remained accessible. The report makes a clear and explicit link between higher education participation, the need to increase skills levels and economic growth:

The risk of failing to expand participation is that we will see a reduction in our standards of living. UKCES [UK Commission for Employment and Skills] analysis suggests that the consequence of failing to increase skills levels is likely to be that the UK gets stuck in a low skill equilibrium, where a substantial part of the economy produces low specification goods and services, which are sold on the basis of low price, and which can only support relatively low paid jobs. (Browne, 2010, p. 17)

So, both 'Higher Ambitions' (BIS, 2009) and the Browne Report (Browne, 2010) suggest either explicitly or by implication that Foundation Degrees may provide a useful means of further developing vocational/professional higher education courses, designed and delivered in collaboration with employers, to widen access, support higher-level skills development and impact upon the economy. Indeed, at the time of writing, the current Minister of State for Universities and Science, David Willets, has also recognized the Foundation Degree as an important part of the strategy for higher education growth within the further education sector and has emphasized the need to see choice and variety (including Foundation Degrees) in terms of further and higher education pathways and qualifications:

Locally-conceived foundation degrees have also been a significant factor in the growth of HE in FE – such that around 10 per cent of all HE now takes place in colleges. What matters most is that there is a range of choice in the market place – Higher National qualifications; professional awards; higher level apprenticeships; foundation, undergraduate and postgraduate degrees – with all necessary information available for employers, employees and students to figure out the best route for them. (Willets, 2011)

Therefore, Foundation Degrees seem to have a role in the future UK further and higher education landscape and are seen by policy makers as part of the strategy to widen participation, improve student choice and the flexibility of provision and increase skill levels.

Summary

In this final chapter, I hope that the reader has been supported in developing a more rounded view of teaching and supporting learning on Foundation Degrees. The chapter has drawn together the issues raised in earlier chapters around learner needs, course design, learning and teaching, e-learning and assessment and has viewed the Foundation Degree student experience holistically, by considering the roles of learner, tutor and workplace and how these roles may act both individually and relationally to potentially enable or inhibit learning. Some examples have been given around specific instances when learning enablement or enhancement has occurred and the discussion has explored ways in which Foundation Degree courses may be designed and delivered to mitigate the learning inhibitors and enhance the learning enablers. Indeed, the key message is that student learning does not happen in isolation, but that many factors may come to bear upon the overall student experience.

Finally, I have suggested that Foundation Degrees have a secure future as part of the further and higher education landscape, as they play an important role in widening access and contributing to skills development for the UK workforce. It is in this context that I wish you well in developing and delivering sustainable, creative, interesting and relevant Foundation Degree courses for potential students now and in the future.

References

Barnett, R. (2007), *A Will to Learn: Being a Student in an Age of Uncertainty*. Buckingham: SRHE/Open University Press.

Billett, S. (2002), 'Toward a workplace pedagogy: guidance, participation and engagement', *Adult Education Quarterly*, 53 (1), 27–43.

BIS (2009), *Higher Ambitions: The Future of Universities in a Knowledge Economy. Executive Summary*. London: BIS. Available online at: www.bis.gov.uk/assets/biscore/corporate/docs/h/09-1452-higher-ambitions-summary.pdf (accessed 12 April 2011).

Boud, D. (2001), 'Knowledge at work: issues of learning', in Boud, D. and Solomon, N. (eds), *Work-Based Learning: A New Higher Education?* Buckingham, UK: SRHE /Open University Press, pp. 34–43.

Bowl, M. (2003), *Non-Traditional Entrants to Higher Education.* Stoke-on-Trent: Trentham Books.

Brennan, L. (2004), 'Making Foundation Degrees work: an introduction and overview', in Brennan, L. and Gosling, D. (eds), *Making Foundation Degrees Work.* London: SEEC, pp. 1–29.

Brennan, L. and Gosling, D. (eds) (2004), *Making Foundation Degrees Work.* London: SEEC.

Browne, J. (2010) *Securing a Sustainable Future for Higher Education: An Independent Review of Higher Education Funding and Student Finance.* Available online at: http://hereview. independent.gov.uk/hereview/ (accessed 12 April 2011).

Darwin, A. (2000), 'Critical reflections on mentoring in work settings', *Adult Education Quarterly*, 50 (3), 197–211.

Duckworth, L. (2006), '"Recycling" Fd early years graduates: strategies for enhancing employer engagement through the training of mentors', *Forward: The Foundation Degree Forward Journal*, 9, 47–48.

Dweck, C. S. (2000), *Self-Theories: Their role in Motivation, Personality and Development.* Philadelphia: Psychology Press.

Fenwick, T. J. (2000), 'Expanding conceptions of experiential learning: a review of five contemporary perspectives on cognition', *Adult Education Quarterly*, 50 (4), 243–272.

Foskett, R. (2003), *Employer and Needs-led Curriculum Planning in Higher Education: A Cross-Sector Case Study of Foundation Degree Development.* Available online at: www. leeds.ac.uk/educol/documents/00003182.htm (accessed 12 January 2009).

Gorard, S., Smith, E., May, H., Thomas, L., Adnett, N. and Slack, K. (2006), 'Review of widening participation research: addressing the barriers to participation in higher education'. A Report to HEFCE by the University of York, Higher Education Academy and Institute for Access Studies. Available online at: www.hefce.ac.uk/pubs/rdreports/2006/rd13_06/barriers.pdf (accessed 16 November 2007).

Green, C. (2006), 'The perceived benefit of work-based learning – capturing the views of students, staff and employers', *Forward: The Foundation Degree Forward Journal*, 9, 27–30.

Gregory, J. (2002), 'Facilitation and facilitator style', in Jarvis, P. (ed.) *The Theory and Practice of Teaching.* London: RoutledgeFalmer, pp. 79–93.

HEFCE (2007), 'Review of widening participation research: addressing the barriers to participation in higher education'. A report to HEFCE by the University of York, Higher Education Academy and Institute for Access Studies. Available online at: www.hefce.ac.uk/pubs/rdreports/2006/rd13_06/barriers.pdf (accessed 30 August 2011).

— (2010), *Foundation Degrees: Key Statistics 2001–02 to 2009–10.* Available online at: www.hefce.ac.uk/pubs/hefce/2010/10_12 (accessed 12 April 2011).

Herde, D. and Rohr, M. (2005), *A Guide to Foundation Degrees.* London: SEEC.

Hockings, C., Cooke, S. and Bowl, M. (2007), '"Academic engagement" within a widening participation context – a 3D analysis', *Teaching in Higher Education*, 12 (5–6), 721–733.

Hulbert, F. (2007), 'The Foundation Degree – nexus complexus', *Forward: The Foundation Degree Forward Journal*, 12, 12–15.

Kolb, D. A. (1984), *Experiential Learning: Experience as the Source of Learning and Development*. New Jersey: Prentice-Hall.

Leitch, S. (2006), *Prosperity for All in the Global Economy – World Class Skills*. Available online at: www.hm-treasury.gov.uk/leitch (accessed 5 April 2008).

Maslow, A. H. (1970), *Motivation and Personality*. (2nd edn). New York: Harper and Row.

Merriam, S., Caffarella, R. and Baumgartner, L. (2007), *Learning in Adulthood: A Comprehensive Guide*. San Francisco: Jossey-Bass.

Mezirow, J. (1997), 'Transformative learning: theory to practice', *New Directions for Adult and Continuing Education*, 74, 5–12.

Moon, J. A. (1999), *Reflection in Learning and Professional Development: Theory and Practice*. London: RoutledgeFalmer.

QAA (2008), *The Framework for Higher Education Qualifications in England, Wales and Northern Ireland (FHEQ)*. Available online at: www.qaa.ac.uk/Publications/InformationAndGuidance/Documents/FHEQ08.pdf (accessed 30 August 2011).

— (2010), *Foundation Degree Qualification Benchmark*. Gloucester: QAA.

Reay, D. (2003), 'Shifting class identities? Social class and the transition to higher education', in Vincent, C. (ed.), *Social Justice, Education and Identity*. London: RoutledgeFalmer, pp. 51–64.

Street, B. V. (1984), *Literacy in Theory and Practice*. Cambridge: Cambridge University Press.

Taylor (2009), 'Learning through a Foundation Degree'. Unpublished PhD thesis. Available online at: http://etheses.nottingham.ac.uk/875/ (accessed 8 April 2011).

Willets, D. (2011), *HE in FE Conference Speech*. London. Available online at: www.bis.gov.uk/news/speeches/david-willetts-aoc-conference-2011 (accessed 12 April 2011).

Yorke, M. and Knight, P. (2004), 'Self-theories: some implications for teaching and learning in higher education', *Studies in Higher Education*, 29 (1), 25–37.

Appendices

Appendix 1

Examples of the typical higher education qualifications at each level of the Framework for Higher Education Qualifications (FHEQ)

Typical higher education qualifications within each level	FHEQ
Doctoral degrees (e.g. PhD/DPhil, EdD, DBA, DClinPsy)	8
Master's degrees (e.g. MPhil, MLitt, MRes, MA, MSc) Integrated master's degrees (e.g. MEng, MChem, MPhys, MPharm) Postgraduate certificates and diplomas Postgraduate certificate in education (PGCE)	7
Bachelor's degrees with honours (e.g. BA/BSc Hons) Bachelor's degrees Professional graduate certificate in education (PGCE) Graduate certificates and diplomas	6
Foundation Degrees (e.g. FdA, FdSc) Diplomas of higher education (DipHE) Higher national diplomas (HND)	5
Higher national certificates (HNC) Certificates of higher education (CertHE)	4

Adapted from QAA (2009).

Appendix 2

Study skills self-assessment

You are beginning your journey into higher education. Your confidence in all these areas will grow as you progress in your studies. However, it can be helpful to identify your current strengths and select some areas for development.

For each of these areas score your confidence from 5 very confident to 1 not confident.

Time management
I know how to:

- break down my work into manageable tasks
- prioritize tasks
- meet deadlines.

Lectures and seminars
I know:

- how to prepare beforehand
- how to work effectively in a group
- what to do when there is something I don't understand.

Library
I know:

- the layout of the library and location of stock for my course
- how to use the library catalogue
- how to access journals and e-resources

Academic reading, referencing and avoiding plagiarism
I know:

- how to find what I'm looking for in articles and book chapters
- how to read actively
- how to identify an author's argument
- how to make, organize and use effective notes
- the importance of referencing and avoiding plagiarism
- how to use the standard referencing system for my subject.

Assessments
I know how to:

- unpack the task
- plan an assignment
- write introductions and conclusions
- write an essay
- write a report
- prepare an oral presentation
- edit and proofread my work
- revise for exams
- use assessment feedback.

Aspects of writing
I know how:

- and when to write in the third person and passive voice
- to write reflectively
- to structure paragraphs
- to structure sentences
- to use punctuation, for example, the apostrophe, the semi-colon.

Study skills action plan

- identify up to three areas you currently feel most confident about
- identify up to three areas in which you would like to develop your confidence
- identify how and when you will work on them.

Strategies might include:

- accessing study skills resources via the virtual learning environment
- looking carefully at texts you are reading to identify the features of academic writing in your subject with a view to incorporating them in your work
- making an appointment with a Learning Developer or course tutor.

Appendix 3

Module specification (pro forma)

Specific guidance for completing this template is available in the Programme Development Manual.

Module title	
Module code	
Module status	[Indicate whether included in single honours/ joint/major/minor and whether core, option or pathway]
Level	
Credits	
Learning hours	
Independent study hours	

RATIONALE

LEARNING OUTCOMES
By the end of the module students are expected to:

SUMMARY OF LEARNING AND TEACHING STRATEGY

SYLLABUS

ASSESSMENT
The module assignment brief will give details related to assignment type and length. The student handbook will contain an overview of overall course assessment.

INDICATIVE READING LIST

- essential reading
- recommended reading.

Appendix 4

Example work-based learning agreement

Foundation degree

Applied studies

Work-based agreement pro-forma for Early Years Key Contact

Thank you for agreeing to support the applicant as a part of his/her degree studies. Your agreement comes under the terms of the University College Code of Practice for Work-Based and Placement Learning.

During the period of the degree the student will be typically working in a setting as an employee or in a voluntary capacity for a minimum of 12 hours per week and there will be a direct link between the student's workplace setting and their studies for the degree.

The University College will have the responsibility for the academic standards and there is no requirement for you to carry out any formal observations, or assessment in the work setting for the degree programme. However, students may require the informal support of a critical friend. This is often dependent on the relationship between the student and Key Contact and therefore, the level of support is negotiable between the student and the Key Contact. A critical friend may be nominated for the student in the workplace who is not necessarily the Key Contact. Support and training for critical friends is provided by the programme team at the University College, please see accompanying information on the roles and responsibilities of critical friends.

NAME OF KEY CONTACT: _____

SETTING: _____

ADDRESS: _____

TELEPHONE: _____

EMAIL: _____

NAME OF CANDIDATE: _____

Additional comments on the suitability of the candidate (if any):

_____

_____

_____

I do support this application.

Signed: _____   Date:

Appendix 5

Writing assessment criteria

Key principles

- Use an outcome-based approach to curriculum design – this focuses on what the student is expected to be able to do by the end of the module or programme.
- This approach uses statements of learning outcomes to express what a learner is expected to know, understand and/or be able to demonstrate at the end of a period of learning. Learning outcomes should be clear and unambiguous and are written in association with level descriptors.
- Assessment criteria specify how threshold performance of the module's learning outcomes are to be demonstrated and should encourage learning at the appropriate level.

Assessment criteria

Assessment criteria describe what the learner is expected to do to show that the learning outcome has been achieved. Be careful not to confuse assessment criteria with the tasks themselves (e.g. 'Write an essay about Karl Marx' is the task). The assessment criteria specify how the task will be assessed.

We use assessment criteria to describe a threshold standard. In this case assessment criteria make it clear to the learner what they have to do to demonstrate that they have achieved the learning outcomes of the module.

How to write assessment criteria

- remember to bear in mind module learning outcomes, the level at which the criteria apply and the nature of the assessment task
- clarity and brevity are important
- language should be clear to all criteria users – students and staff
- the criteria should be capable of being assessed in a valid and reliable way
- the criteria are concerned with the essential aspects of performance for the achievement of a pass.

Appendix 6

Sample assignment brief pro forma

Programme		
The full name of the programme e.g. BA (Hons) Professional Studies		
Level	Module code	Module title
The relevant level of HE study		
Title of assignment		Weighting
This should state the type of assignment (e.g. essay, report, portfolio, presentation). If there is a specific title it may be detailed here		This indicates how much of a module the assessment counts for, e.g. 50%, 100%

Description of task

There should be enough detail here for the task to be completed independently. (Any tutorial support available to support assignment preparation will be made clear by the module team). There should be information about length of assignment; number of tasks (if applicable, e.g. for a portfolio submission); question choices (if applicable); any specific information or literature that must be referred to; and instructions regarding the inclusion of appendices. Depending on the type of assignment, this section may only be a few lines long, or could be a page or more. It should also be clear whether the assignment is to be anonymously marked.

Module outcomes to be tested

Normally there will be between one and five listed. These are exactly the same as those listed in the module specification which appears in the module handbook. If the module has more than one assignment component, it may not be necessary to test all outcomes within each component. Module outcomes are written with the level of study in mind and therefore become more challenging as the programme progresses.

Assessment criteria

The assessment criteria should clearly relate to the module outcomes and give a clear picture of what is expected from the assignment. The assessment criteria will reflect the level of study and describe a threshold standard – this is what the learner is expected to do to demonstrate satisfactory achievement of learning outcomes. The criteria may be divided between all or some of these headings, with the balance of division dependent upon the type of module and assignment.

- knowledge and understanding
- intellectual skills (analysis, synthesis, evaluation and application)
- transferable skills (group working, learning resources, self-evaluation, management of information, autonomy, communication, problem solving)
- practical skills.

Mark scheme

How this is presented will vary a little from programme to programme, but clear principles govern the formation of mark scheme:

- the lowest pass mark (e.g. 40% for undergraduate study) represents a threshold level of achievement at which all assessment criteria have been met
- the mark scheme covers all assessment criteria for the module
- the mark scheme must indicate progressive levels of achievement both above and below threshold level.

The mark scheme can be a useful tool for students to self-assess their progress during assignment preparation.

Date and time of submission
Plagiarism

Note to students: your attention is drawn to the Code of Practice covering plagiarism. Penalties for work found to be plagiarized are severe and can include the withdrawal of the right to resubmit work and termination of studies. On the submission of the assignment you will be required to sign a declaration that the work is your own and that all sources have been properly acknowledged.

Date on which marked work will be available for collection

Programmes must specify a date and publicize any changes to this via the programme notice board or VLE course.

Appendix 7

How to Use Assessment Feedback

This sheet outlines how to recognize and make use of feedback from a variety of sources

All information ©2009 Bishop Grosseteste University College Lincoln

i

What is feedback?
Did you know that feedback can be any of the following...

From your peers

Peer-group feedback associated with peer-assessment

Informal work with peers

Feedback

From your tutors

Word-processed comments about assessed work

A mark or grade given for an assignment or exam

Handwritten comments on returned assessed work

A face-to-face individual tutorial

Written reports on the overall work of a whole group

Face-to-face feedback to groups

Emailed comments on your work

'Tracked changes' on your work

From yourself

Self-assessment – looking back at your work and seeing how you are progressing

Identifiying areas for improvement

Completing self-assessments for hand-in with your assignments

From a mentor or placement supervisor

Formal and informal written or spoken comments during placement

Feedback helps you to...

...identify what you need to do next;

...take action to improve your learning;

...make sense of what you are learning;

...make realistic evaluations of your achievements;

...reflect on your past work in ways you can use to improve future work.

What should you do with feedback?

1. Read or listen to feedback carefully

2. Ensure you understand what is written or said

3. Use it!

YOU need to find the most effective way of using feedback so that you can build on your strengths and identify areas where you may need to improve

Tips on how to use feedback

- keep assignment feedback sheets together (you may already do this within your PDP) – this will help you to identify common themes

- look back over your feedback sheets – do the same or similar comments recur? What can you do to address common issues? Look at the Blackboard Learning Advice site for help

- re-read you feedback sheets before your next assignment as this may help you achieve a better standard next time

- re-read the assignment as well as your feedback, so that your feedback is in context

- take action from your feedback – these prompts may help...

One thing I'm going to do is...	In future, I'm not going to...
I'm going to think more about...	An easy thing to fix is...
I have found out that ...	I need to find out more about...
I'd like to know ...	

Index

Page numbers in **bold** denote figures/tables.